ROTH MEMORY COURSE

A SIMPLE AND SCIENTIFIC METHOD OF IMPROVING
THE MEMORY AND INCREASING
MENTAL POWER

By DAVID M. ROTH

THE SEVEN LESSONS

ONE . . . . FIFTY-WORD FOUNDATION
TWO . . . . MENTAL FILING
THREE . . . . NAMES AND FACES
FOUR . . . . HOW TO READ AND A B C MEMORY CODE
FIVE . . . . NUMBERS
SIX . . . . MEMORY AIDS FOR STUDY
SEVEN . . . . PRACTICAL APPLICATIONS

RALSTON PUBLISHING CO.
CLEVELAND, OHIO

Copyright, 1918
Copyright, 1934
By
DAVID M. ROTH

All rights reserved, including that of translation into foreign
languages, including the Scandinavian

PRINTED IN THE UNITED STATES OF AMERICA

CL

Printing Statement:

Due to the very old age and scarcity of this book, many of the pages may be hard to read due to the blurring of the original text, possible missing pages, missing text and other issues beyond our control.

Because this is such an important and rare work, we believe it is best to reproduce this book regardless of its original condition.

Thank you for your understanding.

DAVID M. ROTH

INTRODUCTION

WHAT did you forget to do today?
And can you remember which day last week it was that you *meant* to phone someone, or write a note, or stop by the store on your way home—but it slipped your mind?

Isn't it exasperating, the way your memory fails you every so often? "What was the name of those people I met last night?" . . . "Why *can't* I think of the title of that book?" . . . "Why do so many *useless* details clutter up my mind, when I can never remember the facts, faces, figures, ideas, names, words and spelling that I need—*when* I need them?"

Does that sound like YOU?

Wouldn't you like to be able to remember each fact you want right at the split-second moment you want it? Think what it would mean to you every day of your life! Imagine the value of having every bit of important information you see or hear filed away accurately, indelibly in your memory—so that you could mentally "put your finger on it" in an instant!

And the remarkable thing about it is—you CAN have a memory exactly like that!

The Roth Memory Course, in seven simple little books, CAN and WILL improve your memory. The first lesson will convince you. Devote just one hour to it and we feel confident that your memory will show marked improvement at once.

THE PUBLISHERS.

THE ROTH MEMORY COURSE

Just a Word as We Start

THIS course will equip your memory, and therefore your mind, to accomplish greater things with less effort than you ever dreamed possible.

Just as a hammer or any other tool in a man's hand is really an extension of the hand, so your better memory will be an extension of your mind.

Like any other tool, whether it be a hammer or a battleship, your mental power is largely wasted unless you learn how to use it.

To learn my method is so easy, so swift, so certain and so free from hard work that it is like a fascinating game.

Any man, woman, boy or girl of average intelligence can possess quickly an accurate memory. It does not take a genius to be a master of the memory. It is all very simple, as I shall show you.

I am going to show this to you in the first lesson.

We will now jump into practical work without further introduction so that you may grasp right at the start the simple basic principle of my method. In one hour or less you will be speeding pleasantly along the road to Better Memory.

We are cleared for action!

DAVID M. ROTH.

LESSON ONE

How to Gain a Good Memory

The Unreliable Memory

"I forgot!"

You have said it thousands of times with embarrassment, vexation, and self-reproach. In attempting to remember speeches, price lists, studies, statistics, names, and faces you have depended on the old, tiresome method of repetition to stamp them on your memory—and it went back on you at the critical moment.

This is all unnecessary. You have the proper mental equipment, but neglect and wrong methods have caused it to deteriorate.

Your memory is actually the most wonderful instrument in the world. You need only to know how to *use* it to do things that appear marvelous. The purpose of these lessons is to afford you a real opportunity for improvement.

The Use of the Law of Association

We can remember only through relation, through association of ideas, because that is the way the normal human mind works, and no one can change it.

Practically all mental action and development are based on the Association of Ideas and the use of the visual faculty.

You know how the talking machine record is made. A sound presses a needle into a moving wax, forming a path. Later, when another needle passes through this recorded path, the same sound is duplicated.

Your brain is a record. The five senses are needles that carry impressions to the brain and form what are called *brain paths*.

When these paths are deep enough, you remember. When they are too faint, you forget. I am going to show you how to make these idea paths deep enough so that they will co-operate with one another. Then you will be able to recall what you now have trouble in remembering. *In other words, you are going to learn to associate and to visualize your ideas.*

You Have the Necessary Faculty

Nature has endowed *one* of your senses with a greater capacity for impressing the brain than any of the others. *An impression made on the brain by the sense of sight is many times stronger than one made there by any of the other senses.* The use of the sense of sight is by far the most necessary if you are to make strong, lasting impressions upon your brain.

The Mind's Eye

Eye-pictures are the most accurate of mental impressions. And because the mind has this wonderful ability to see pictures long after the disappearance of the original pictures that the real eye made on the mind, we speak of the *mind's eye*, and of seeing in our *mind's eye*. The scientific name for the *mind's eye* is *Visualization*, and the ability to use this wonderful faculty is invaluable to you.

LESSON ONE

Through Visualization You Will Learn to Remember

In these lessons I shall teach you how to visualize—to make mind pictures at will. By using these mind pictures in a definite, systematic way you will learn to remember. This visual faculty is developed easily by following the natural methods in these lessons.

Visual Imagination Strengthened

In these lessons I ask you to imagine some things that at first may strike you as unusual. Yet they are not, and they would not seem so to the average child because he has been using his imagination and giving it free play.

I ask you to do the same. I want you to begin by awakening your imagination, if you have allowed it to lie dormant. By its invaluable aid you will learn to form pictures that will be impressed on the memory.

Memory is the ability to recall at will impressions made upon the mind. If we cannot recall impressions we are said to have forgotten them.

In order to revive your impressions you must make them strong enough for ready recall.

There are three natural principles of mental operation to which I now call your attention, and by which you will make visual impressions strong enough to recall easily. This will be to *remember*.

I. The First Aid Is Exaggeration

Exaggeration is mentally to enlarge, or magnify the objects or incidents to more than their actual proportions. For instance, if you see a cow in a field you will be more likely to hold the impression, if your imagination makes you *see* the cow as large as an elephant.

This is the idea used by the cartoonist. You see it used in advertising, on billboards and in many different ways and take it as a matter of course. You are so accustomed to seeing these distorted pictures that even the artist's extreme exaggeration does not strike you as unusual. This is what *you* must learn to do with your imagination. *At times be a cartoonist with the things you wish to remember.* Enlarge them to unusual and unnatural proportions if necessary.

Exaggeration is a most practical principle, and the use of it enables us to make lasting impressions on the mind.

II. The Second Aid Is Motion

Motion—The mind has always been strongly attracted to motion of every kind. Children like to see the wheels go around. If you have a friend in a crowd you can get his attention by waving your hand. Some-

Lesson One

thing moving in a show-window will always attract the passers-by. A person lacking in the power of concentration will focus his closest attention upon a moving

picture or object. Just as motion pictures are more attractive than the old style stereopticon views, so motion —put into the pictures that you are going to learn to form—will increase the power of the mind to retain and to recall them.

III. The Third Aid Is Unusual Associations

Unusual Associations—It is the occurrences in life that are out of the ordinary, unusual, and different from what we are in the habit of seeing, that impress us strongly. At night we relate to those at home the *unusual* happenings of the day.

Take advantage of the fact that things out of the ordinary impress us more than those that are commonplace. In order to retain your visual associations you must make them unusual. Some of us find it necessary to make these associations grotesque and ludicrous, although I do not recommend the extreme use of this.

There is no limit to the use of Exaggeration, Motion, or the Unusual, in forming your mental views.

You can realize this fully by glancing over the advertising illustrations in magazines, and the cartoons in the daily papers.

You can picture a HAT or a HIVE the size of a mountain, a NAIL the height of a telephone pole. You can picture it moving, swinging, falling, or flying.

You are now going to use your mind in the new—the *visual*—way.

You will be familiar quickly with a series of objects that it would be difficult to remember through ordinary forms of association.

They have been selected because in most instances they do not form ready associations with one another. But now see what the picture-making power of your mind will do for you.

The First Visual Picture

The first object I wish you to see is a HAT. Pay no attention to the letters H-A-T, but call before the *mind's eye* the visual image of the HAT. Actually see this HAT. Let it be a large, black, shiny HAT. See it clearly, the sheen of the silk, the ribbon, the upturned brim. See it in a definite place—on the floor, chair or table, or suspended in midair.

Lesson One

The visual ability will come to you quickly—do not feel discouraged if at first you do not see the HAT clearly in your mind.

It will probably help you to close your eyes while forming these *Mental* pictures. Draw or outline the HAT or do anything that will assist you to see the HAT with the *mind's eye*.

Need of Exaggeration

If you find it difficult to recall your picture of the HAT, you can strengthen the impression by exaggerating the size of the HAT. See it, not in normal size, but three or four times as large.

You can enlarge it to still greater proportions if you need to. You can see the HAT the size of a house. The larger your imagination pictures the HAT the stronger the impression will be.

Also Use Motion

As you watch the HAT see it move up and down as if controlled by some hidden thread. You may see it blown about by the wind. This is a common sight in city streets. See the HAT in motion.

These methods will fix the picture of the HAT in mind and enable you to make the impression as strong as you choose.

To Impress Many Objects

To fix in mind a list of objects it is merely necessary to use the same principle, except that you will apply it now to *two* objects instead of one. You will make a *mind's-eye* picture of the two objects together.

Attend carefully while I describe for you a series of pictures that will include words selected with care for definite purposes, as explained in this and following lessons.

Do not merely *read* these descriptions. Your *mind's eye* should *see* every picture clearly.

I. The First Combination Picture

To the HAT which we have pictured, we will now add a HEN. You must see the HAT and the HEN together. See both objects clearly. Enlarge them. See a large HEN strutting about wearing the HAT. Here is an illustration combining these two objects.

Probably your imagination has formed a picture of your own. If not, impress the drawing on this page on your *mind's eye*. See the HEN moving about, very proud of her new possession, the HAT. Or see the HEN making her nest in the HAT. But be sure and *see* a picture of some kind in your *mind's eye*, combining the HAT and the HEN.

II. Hen and Ham

Add to the HEN, HAM. See a big HAM out in the yard. The large HEN runs and jumps on the HAM and dances a jig there. Work with the picture by the above methods until you see it clearly.

LESSON ONE 9

See the objects larger than usual. Have them exaggerated out of proportion. Actually see the motion.

See, if possible, a HEN of some distinct color, a red or a white HEN, and a definite picture of a whole HAM or a slice of HAM.

See only two objects—HEN and HAM—do not see the HAT in this picture. See two objects and only two in each picture. As you add the new one —HAM—you drop the first object—HAT—and see only the HEN and the HAM.

III. Ham and Hare

Add to the HAM, HARE. See the HAM on the ground being pushed and rolled along by the HARE. It is hard work for the HARE. See him exerting all his strength to move the HAM. See clearly the HAM and the HARE.

IV. Hare and Hill

Add to the HARE, HILL. See the HARE scampering down the HILL as fast as he can run. Every now and then he turns his head in fright to see if he is being followed. See clearly the HARE running down the HILL.

Make Clear Pictures

The ability to retain visual impressions depends upon the clearness with which you actually *see* the objects.

Try now to increase the vividness of every visual impression.

Important—You must see only two of these objects in every picture.

V. Hill and Shoe

See a steep HILL, or a mountainside which you will consider a HILL. As you watch the top of the HILL an object appears to drop from the sky, alighting on the HILL. It is a large, dilapidated SHOE—a giant's SHOE. You readily recall the big shoe in the picture of the "old lady who lived in a shoe." Use a SHOE of this size in your picture. See it sliding down the HILL.

VI. Shoe and Cow

See the SHOE which is moving rapidly strike a COW grazing in a pasture. The poor COW is badly frightened. She throws up her heels and runs away.

VII. Cow and Hive

Add to the COW, HIVE. See the COW, either a new COW, or the same COW, as in the previous picture. She is still running, and spies a large HIVE. With lowered head she charges the HIVE, striking it with her horns.

VIII. Hive and Ape

To HIVE add APE. See the upturned HIVE rolling about, until finally a large APE comes out and looks about in a dazed sort of way.

LESSON ONE 11

IX. Ape and Woods

The APE sees a WOODS near by. See him climb the trees and swing from one branch to another.

Now go back and see again your first *mind's-eye* picture. Name aloud the objects that this picture contains. Thus:

Hat and Hen

You have two pictures with the HEN in them, and the HEN in the first picture will easily and naturally bring to your mind the HEN of the second picture.

Your picture of HEN will then bring to mind the new object, the HAM. Close your book and go over all the other pictures in the same manner, naming both objects in each picture.

Our Memory Movies
Nine Pictures—Ten Objects

If you have clearly visualized the pictures as I have described them, you have without difficulty recalled this list of ten objects, thus:

```
1—HAT  and HEN
2—HEN  and HAM
3—HAM  and HARE
4—HARE and HILL
5—HILL and SHOE
6—SHOE and COW
7—COW  and HIVE
8—HIVE and APE
9—APE  and WOODS
```

Review this list of words by this picture method a number of times until they come easily, quickly, and accurately before you.

If you find that one picture does not come as easily as the others, stop a moment. If you do not see the COW and the HIVE as quickly and as readily as you can see the SHOE and the COW, introduce into this picture of COW and HIVE more exaggeration or motion.

See a huge HIVE. Let it be moved rapidly or fly through space after the COW has struck it. See it more clearly. Then review, and you will probably recall this picture as easily as any.

The pictures that I have described have been merely suggestions to give your imagination a start. Should other pictures present themselves to you, either imaginative or actual scenes from the past, by all means use them—your own pictures—if they appeal to you—but do not make them too commonplace.

Throughout this and subsequent lessons always follow the pictures suggested by your own mind—provided you are able to recall them successfully. No two minds operate alike. Every individual will form different pictures.

It is important to make a proper start. Learning to visualize will have a direct bearing on your future progress. I will describe briefly other pictures that might be as good as the original illustration of HAM and HARE, or even better.

Select Some Picture

You may choose any of the pictures that I have described or, preferably, one of your own. If you have difficulty some one of the following suggestions may aid you in forming your pictures.

Lesson One

Five Ways to Link Ham and Hare

See the HARE with the HAM tied to its back, like a pack horse.

The HARE may be seen dragging or pulling the HAM.

The HARE may have the HAM tied to its tail as a tin can is tied to a dog's tail. The HARE may be pictured much larger than the HAM, or vice versa.

The HAM may be hollow and the HARE may be seen hiding in it and timidly peeping out, or the HARE may be hiding back of the HAM.

The HARE may be seen eating a slice of HAM.

Use any of these pictures if you prefer, instead of the first described picture of the HARE rolling the HAM.

Complete the List

In the same manner as before form pictures of the following objects. Use your imagination. Make the scenes unusual. Form moving pictures. Enlarge the objects. See but two objects in every picture.

Woods and Tide

See the WOODS on the edge of a body of water that we picture as the TIDE. See the waves breaking along the shore, and the spray dashing on the trees of the WOODS.

Tide and Tin

See a large sheet of TIN, or a large TIN can, floating on the TIDE. Stop a moment until you have visualized the picture clearly and accurately.

Tin and Team

Bring exaggeration into play. This TIN is so heavy it takes a TEAM to move it. Try and see the TEAM clearly and note their color.

Team and Tire

See the TEAM frightened by a large TIRE rolling toward them. Note the advertisements of TIRE companies and see how successfully the artists have used these same elements of imagination and exaggeration.

Form Your Own Pictures

Now proceed through the list and make your own pictures. Stop a moment between every pair of words and see the picture clearly. Make one clear *mind's eye* picture of the two objects and pass on.

Do not wonder whether these pictures will revive—just continue along with me. See each one clearly for a moment, then on to the next.

TIRE   and HOTEL
HOTEL and DISH
DISH   and DOG
DOG   and DOVE
DOVE   and TUB
TUB   and NOSE

Review again the pictures that you made, beginning with WOODS, calling aloud the names of the two objects in every picture.

See them clearly. Try, until you can recall them very

Lesson One 15

clearly, improving your pictures or putting in more exaggeration or motion, if they prove difficult to recall.

Without looking at the list go back now to HAT and call the words in pairs.

>1—HAT and HEN
>2—HEN and HAM
>3—HAM and HARE

Having repeated all the words in this manner from HAT to NOSE, go over the list again, omitting the word *and*.

Be sure to *see* your pictures and to call every word from HAT to NOSE singly, thus: HAT, HEN, HAM, HARE, HILL, SHOE, COW, HIVE, APE, WOODS, TIDE, etc.

You Can Go Backward or Forward

After doing this a few times, you will be able to reverse the process.

Go slowly from NOSE backward to HAT.

First say

>NOSE and TUB
>TUB and DOVE
>DOVE and DOG

Then go back again from NOSE, and as you recall the pictures repeat the words singly, NOSE, TUB, DOVE, DOG, DISH, HOTEL, etc.

You can also begin in the middle and go either way you wish.

Begin at TIN and go backward, recalling every picture until you reach HAT. Then, again, starting with TIN go forward to NOSE.

This Practice is Valuable—Continue It

Proceed as before to add to your picture gallery.

NOSE   and WINDOW
WINDOW and NUN
NUN   and GNOME
GNOME   and SNARE
SNARE   and NAIL

Here is a good opportunity for exaggeration. See the NAIL of huge size. Then

NAIL   and HINGE
HINGE and INK
INK   and KNIFE
KNIFE and KNOB
KNOB   and MOOSE

Be sure that you form a clear picture of every combination. See the objects large and in motion—make your pictures as unusual as you can.

Now review your pictures. First in pairs, beginning with NOSE—

1—NOSE   and WINDOW
2—WINDOW and NUN, etc.

Then repeat them as a list without the repetition, thus:

Nose, Window, Nun, Gnome, Snare

Now repeat them backward, beginning with MOOSE and back to NOSE.

LESSON ONE 17

Another Ten Words

MOOSE and MUD
MUD and MOON
MOON and MUMMY
MUMMY and HAMMER
HAMMER and MULE
MULE and MATCH
MATCH and HAMMOCK
HAMMOCK and MUFF
MUFF and MOP
MOP and ROSE

You will soon be able to form visual impressions of any kind instantaneously, but take enough time now to make a clear picture in every instance.

Stop here and review forward and backward, as before.

Another Series

ROSE and RAT
RAT and RAIN
RAIN and RAM
RAM and WARRIOR
WARRIOR and RAIL
RAIL and ROACH
ROACH and RAKE
RAKE and ROOF
ROOF and ROPE
ROPE and LACE

Review your scenes from ROSE to LACE, then from LACE backward to ROSE.

Now recall every picture, beginning with HAT and ending with LACE.

See the Picture before You Speak

Do not repeat the words by heart. You must *see* the pictures to gain real benefit from this practice.

After you have gone from HAT to LACE begin with LACE and trace your scenes backward to HAT, calling every word as you see the object.

Important

Do not form new pictures every time you go through the list. See the ones you first made. Every time you recall your picture make it more distinct.

Code Words

HAT	TIDE	WINDOW	MUD	RAT
HEN	TIN	NUN	MOON	RAIN
HAM	TEAM	GNOME	MUMMY	RAM
HARE	TIRE	SNARE	HAMMER	WARRIOR
HILL	HOTEL	NAIL	MULE	RAIL
SHOE	DISH	HINGE	MATCH	ROACH
COW	DOG	INK	HAMMOCK	RAKE
HIVE	DOVE	KNIFE	MUFF	ROOF
APE	TUB	KNOB	MOP	ROPE
WOODS	NOSE	MOOSE	ROSE	LACE

A Good Start

Now let us take a bird's-eye view of what you have accomplished.

You have learned a series of fifty words that you can repeat forward and backward. They are all unassociated, yet you have formed a chain of pictures whereby you have learned the words in a new and interesting way instead of by the old, cumbersome method of repetition.

Having learned these fifty words in picture form, you may compliment yourself on an excellent start towards the goal of a better memory.

A New Way

You have begun to remember in a new way. You have really learned the alphabet of my method. Make these fifty words just as much a part of your mental equipment as the alphabet.

Go back and read pages 8 to 16 several times until you are thoroughly familiar with this method of using your mind. Be sure not to form new pictures every time you go over the list. Review the same pictures every time.

Form Large Pictures

In the beginning learn to see things in large proportions. Introduce motion even into pictures of inanimate objects.

This requires what you may consider a stretch of your imagination, but it will accomplish results, and is necessary only in the beginning. It revives a mental faculty that, before long, will operate with rapidity and accuracy.

You must have two objects in every picture. Do not make the mistake of forming a picture of only one object at a time.

Two Objects in Every Picture

You cannot make any progress this way, as it will be impossible for you to pass from one picture to the next. Always associate *two,* and only two, objects in every picture. Do not have the HAT, HEN and HAM all in the same picture.

Your first picture is one of the HAT and the HEN.

Then a picture of the HEN and a HAM. Next the HAM and a HARE.

Every picture will recall the next, because every object is part of two pictures, with the exception of the HAT and the LACE.

Review these pictures several times every day, for a few days. You will then be able to retain the list as long as wanted, an occasional recall being all that is necessary.

Visualization Applied

The visual principle has been applied by many students immediately after the first lesson.

One business man testified that he had never remembered the simple errands for his wife.

The day after his first lesson she requested him to bring home two cans of milk, some toothpicks, and a file. He pictured two large cans of milk in front of the grocery, built a barricade of toothpicks around them, and laid a file over the top.

He couldn't forget this.

A department store owner wanted to order a special table from a factory, and also to speak to one of his buyers.

He formed a mental picture of the table, on which the buyer was seated, blocking the door of his office. Such pictures usually do the work.

Learn the Fifty Words Thoroughly

I realize that unless you are naturally a good visualizer, it has been necessary to make some effort to form some of these pictures. You have the ability. *A little practice daily is all that is required.* You will remember you did not learn to write, to add, to subtract, or to multiply in a day or a week. You built all your knowledge a bit at a time.

Rewards in Store

So I caution you again to learn these fifty words thoroughly so that you will have a good foundation for the rest of the lessons. It will bring you as great a reward as the ability to read or to figure. Your memory will improve faster all the time, and you will understand the truth contained in Dr. James's statement that the average business man uses but a small percentage of his normal mental capacity. Application *now* will make your mind pay cash dividends.

Put Some Fun into Your Practice

Don't make a grind out of this practice.

After you have learned your list of fifty words there is a chance for recreation.

Ask a friend to give you a list of ten, fifteen, or more words. Tell him to write down a list of *objects* in the room and to tell you every word as he writes it. Later on you can take longer and more difficult words as easily.

Surprise Your Friends

As the list is given to you, visualize every two objects together, just as you did HAT and HEN. Make large pictures and see them clearly. Then repeat the list to him, forward and backward. It will surprise your friend and exercise your mind.

If you have children, give them in simple language a knowledge of the principles of this lesson.

No Limit to Memory Capacity

Improving the memory does not mean burdening it. There is no limit to its capacity. On the contrary, use and exercise of the memory make it easier to remember.

The memory is not a storehouse whose contents are limited. The memory is simply one use of the mind. The mind contains billions of brain cells, only a part of which is actually used. Put the dormant tracts into operation. That is what these lessons will do for you.

Importance of the Code Words

In the lessons to follow, you will make practical use of the code words.

You will be surprised at the help these words will give you, so learn them thoroughly.

They will be of aid in remembering telephone numbers, addresses, price lists, and figures of all kinds. They also have many other valuable uses, as you will see.

LESSON ONE 23

SUMMARY

1. Use of Association

2. The Mind's Eye

3. Visual Imagination

4. Three Natural Memory Aids
    1. Exaggeration
    2. Motion
    3. Unusual Associations

5. Our Mental Movies

6. Form Clear Pictures

7. Fifty Pictorial Code Words

8. Review the Pictures Forward and Backward

9. See Your Pictures Before You Speak the Words

10. Two Objects in Every Picture

11. How to Put Some Fun Into Your Practice

12. Code Words Will Be Useful. Learn Them

HOW I DISCOVERED AN EASY WAY TO REMEMBER

How I Began

When I was a young man my memory was below normal. It was because my memory was so wretched that I determined to find some way to cure the trouble.

It did not take me long to discover that a bad memory is not so much a matter of forgetting as of not *getting* at all.

In other words, the pictures made on the brain were blurred, indistinct, foggy.

This applied to facts, figures, names, and faces—all of which slipped from my mind because my mind had never really taken a firm *hold* on them.

I might be introduced to a man and in twenty seconds would realize that I had forgotten his name.

My *ears* had heard the name spoken, my *eyes* had seen his face, but my *brain* had failed to register any picture of either or to connect the two permanently.

So with my work in high school—I seemed to grasp what I heard and read, without trouble—perhaps too easily—but I did not grip it fast.

It went into one ear and out of the other.

Here, then, was the trouble—the *lenses* of my senses did not *focus* sharp pictures on my brain.

My mental images were so weak, shallow, diffused or confused that they would not reproduce when I called for them.

How I Succeeded

The memory systems that have been taught seemed to me too complex, too difficult, too much like drudgery, and lacking in practical effectiveness. Some of them were valuable to men of exceptional brain capacity and education, but I had no exceptional brain. It was just average, nothing more.

But I had to do something, because my poor memory was too heavy a handicap for me to succeed.

So I set about evolving a method of my own to supply my own great need. I worked along simple, natural, yet scientific lines.

It proved effective. I was astonished at the progress I made in improving my memory.

I explained this method to my friends. It helped them as much as it did me.

It was through the enthusiasm and insistence of my friends that I was practically forced into making memory training my life work.

As I said before, I do not believe that any normal man had a worse memory than I, particularly in the matter of names.

Now, fifty or a hundred persons in an audience may rise, one after the other, every one telling me his name. While my back is turned, they may all change seats to different parts of the hall. Then I can call each man by name.

People gasp when I do such things; yet with the simple memory system I have devised, any one of them, with a little application, can learn to accomplish even more difficult feats.

I have met more than ten thousand people in the last few years, from Seattle to New York, and believe that I could meet almost any one of them unexpectedly and call him by name.

How You Can Succeed

You can do the same things if you will apply yourself to my memory method. You master it in a few lessons, and that mastery is not a matter of knitted brows and throbbing temples; it is *fun,* like an exciting game; it quickens your whole being while you are teaching your memory to work.

I often ask the audience to call out twenty or more numbers of three figures each while somebody writes them down where I cannot see them. Then I not only repeat the entire list backward or forward, but tell instantly which is the eighth or seventeenth or any other number, and I give the figures located at any point in the list.

You can shuffle a deck of cards and call out the fifty-two cards to me quite rapidly; I will recite the cards in their order, backward or forward. I not only will repeat without an error, but will give the number of any card, counting from the top, or the card for any number.

There is no trick about this at all. It is the straightforward work of the trained memory, and you can do it as successfully as I.

I can tell you the day of the week for any date for two hundred years back, or in the coming centuries. Give me your birth date and I will tell you at once the day of the week on which you were born.

You can learn to perform this amazing feat in a few hours' time, and by occasional rehearsals can become so skilled that you can give the answer almost instantly. So you see it is not amazing at all—except that the human mind is amazing if used correctly.

The remarkable thing is that so few persons come anywhere near to a full realization of their mental possibilities. It is simply a matter of *knowing how.*

Why You Should Succeed

An accurate, retentive memory is the basis of all business success. Without it one may count pretty surely on failure from the start, no matter what university diploma one may have on one's wall.

Business men realize this—or are beginning to—and that is why I have been invited to address the leading business men's organizations in the largest cities, from Seattle to New York.

Remember that if my Memory Course were confined to the teaching of memory feats it would never have secured the standing among practical business and professional men that it has.

The Importance of a Reliable Memory

The business world has awakened to the tremendous importance of memory. It has realized that an unreliable memory is a great handicap.

Memory is the basis of education, progress, and success. The most necessary intellectual qualities of the business man are judgment and imagination. Without memory there could be no judgment or constructive planning power.

Judgment Based on Memory

A sound judgment is the result of weighing the knowledge and evidence stored in the mind. The more knowledge you bring to bear on the subject the more accurate will be the judgment.

The successful man is the one who is able to classify and file away in the mind his experiences and the experiences of others. He is able to recall these experiences when needed in reaching conclusions.

Thus we see that only what we remember of our past experiences is of any value in winning success.

Cause of Failures

The majority of failures in the business world are due to poor judgment on the part of business men. The cause back of these failures is the inability of the mind to retain the facts and experiences necessary to lead the mind to sound judgment.

Memory Training Neglected

The effect of all efforts toward education is limited entirely by the capacity of the student's memory. Despite its importance, improving the memory, has been sadly neglected. Although it is the basis of all learning, little attempt has been made by our educational institutions to strengthen this faculty.

Memory Can Be Improved

This is due largely to the mistaken idea that memory is a gift. On the contrary, a good memory is usually the result of training based upon correct principles.

Within the past few years it has been proved that memory training is necessary to satisfactory progress in learning.

Memory can be depended upon to an amazing degree. The average man has no conception of its possibilities because he rarely gives it a chance to serve him.

You Can Be the Exceptional Man

Progress can be made only by the trained mind: Instead of letting your unreliable memory hold you back, you should control your mental powers and advance to big achievements.

The business world pays the large salary to the man with the trained mind.

Train your mind to remember, and you can be the exceptional man.

An Exceptional Memory—Not the Exception but the Rule

An army maxim says that a good captain will not ask his men to do anything he will not do. I have developed my own memory and the memories of thousands of students from an average or sub-average quality up to what the business world calls an exceptional memory. *The application of the principles of these lessons results in a mental development beyond belief.* Indeed, many pupils bid fair to outstrip their teacher.

Endorsements

Business and professional men enthusiastically endorse this Memory Course, and are using it daily. They know—and you can know—that the information in these lessons, confidently applied, makes an exceptional memory—not the exception—but the rule.

With the aid of the practical method I have evolved, you will be able to do wonderful things in the course of a few weeks.

You will be able to remember names and faces, statistics, facts, and other information.

Every statement, every suggestion, every hint in these lessons is Experience—boiled down.

Follow the suggestions in this first lesson. There are practical applications in it that you can use in your daily life. Grasp them and you will at once begin to understand the wonderful chance for the development of your memory. You will learn how quickly information can be recorded and how certainly it can be retained.

A Great Authority

Professor William James, in his great *Psychology*, says: "The more other facts a fact is associated with in the mind, the better possession of it our memory retains. . . . The one who *thinks* over his experiences most, and weaves them into systematic relations with each other, will be the one with the best memory."

You have noticed that a voice, or a scene, will often recall a train of events that carry your mind back to childhood days. A song brings up the scene where you first heard it. A scent may recall a face. A book, or an old picture, bring back something long forgotten.

The sound, or the picture, made a deep path at the time, although you did not know it. These impressions on your mind have remained. Like a flash of lightning your mental operations go back along these impressions from now to then—and you remember.

The Eye and the Brain

The pictures that pass through the eye—along the eye nerves to be impressed upon the brain—are the most enduring of all the sensations that reach the brain through any of the five senses. You remember what you *see*.

Lesson One

much longer than what you hear, feel, taste, or smell.

From your earliest childhood, probably without knowing it, you have been learning and remembering by what you saw.

In childhood your mind was more ready for impressions. And of all impressions, the eyes made the deepest brain paths.

Old people who cannot remember the happenings of yesterday can tell you in detail the stories of their youth. Such stories are almost invariably of things they saw.

There are people who are born with exceptional ability to form mental pictures. History tells of many who could read a page and then repeat, word for word, line for line, everything printed on the page.

You may remember some of your schoolmates who could read their lesson once and then make an almost perfect recitation.

They were able to record the page on the mind at one reading. Later, the *mind's eye* could see the text while the lips were repeating it. They were excellent visualizers.

Good visualizers should do their utmost to develop the faculty—it is priceless. But those who lack it need not despair, for it can be developed. This you will prove for yourself as you make progress with this lesson, and with those to follow.

I do not intend to teach you to photograph the page mentally, but rather to impress certain *pictures* on your mind by the use of your *imagination*.

Your Imagination

Speaking frankly, I believe that many people are ashamed of one of the greatest gifts the Creator has given us—the imagination. Or, if not actually ashamed, they are reluctant about using it. Every child naturally has a good imagination. Parents frequently throw cold water on what is perhaps the fire of genius. They say "Oh, he is always imagining things!" or "She is a dreamy sort of child, not at all practical."

Common sense is a good thing. But no one ever invented, made, or won anything unless he used his *imagination* first. Common sense is the fuel. Imagination is the match that makes it flame into deeds.

Efficiency is a necessity—one of the great things that has come into modern business. But the big man of the future must be more than a super-efficient man. He must be a man of great *vision*—of *trained imagination*.

Every great invention—the steam engine, the cotton gin, the telegraph, the telephone, the electric light, the wireless, the submarine, the aeroplane, the radio—had first to be imagined before it came into being.

And every one of these, almost every step in human progress, was ridiculed as a silly absurdity.

Co-operate

1. *Take these lessons seriously.* Learn every step as I outline it—not as you think it ought to be learned.

2. *Practice.* Be sincere with me. But, more important, be sincere with yourself. Unless you supply the will I cannot supply the way. And I am sincerely desirous of doing that.

3. *Follow instructions carefully*—and you will have personal proof that this course is a pleasure-giving, money-making education for you.

Code Words Are a Valuable Key

I have told you several times that it is important for you to learn the code words. In addition to giving you needed exercise, they are the basis for a mental file that will enable you to store any information you wish to retain.

The code words also will furnish you an infallible key for remembering numbers. You will find all this interesting, easy and, above all, absolutely practical.

As We Go Forward

In the next lesson the tremendous value of the code words will be brought home to you.

Immediately you will begin to make use of them.

You will see how easily you can hang up ideas in your mind, as easily, as neatly, as conveniently, as you hang up your hat.

Remembering unusual activities, engagements, errands, anything you should do will be as easy as remembering to open your mail or anything you do from habit.

Then comes the all important remembering of names and faces. This is one of the biggest lessons and the practical value of it cannot be over-estimated.

It does not matter how treacherous your memory is for names. It can be no worse than mine was, for remember I could scarcely retain a name for twenty seconds.

Now there are more than 10,000 men and women whom I believe I can call by name on sight, whether I meet them in Seattle, New York or any other place.

PRACTICE CHART 1

Recall your picture associations for the following code words. To the left, write the word which precedes the code word—to the right, the word which follows the code word. Note example: *Dish* precedes DOG—*Dove* follows DOG.

Dish	Dog	*Dove*	_____	Roof	_____
_____	Cow	_____	_____	Muff	_____
_____	Ham	_____	_____	Hare	_____
_____	Rat	_____	_____	Tide	_____
_____	Mud	_____	_____	Rake	_____
_____	Tub	_____	_____	Team	_____
_____	Ape	_____	_____	Mule	_____
_____	Mop	_____	_____	Rope	_____
_____	Ink	_____	_____	Moon	_____
_____	Nun	_____	_____	Nose	_____
_____	Tin	_____	_____	Hinge	_____
_____	Ram	_____	_____	Snare	_____
_____	Hen	_____	_____	Hotel	_____
_____	Rail	_____	_____	Knife	_____
_____	Dish	_____	_____	Roach	_____
_____	Hive	_____	_____	Gnome	_____
_____	Rose	_____	_____	Woods	_____
_____	Hill	_____	_____	Match	_____
_____	Nail	_____	_____	Moose	_____
_____	Tire	_____	_____	Mummy	_____
_____	Shoe	_____	_____	Window	_____
_____	Dove	_____	_____	Hammer	_____
_____	Knob	_____	_____	Warrior	_____
_____	Rain	_____	_____	Hammock	_____

LESSON TWO

How to Train the Memory For Every-Day Needs

Everybody Needs Memory Training

The methods in these lessons will give you a useful memory.

The simplest facts slip away from the average memory—facts that have been learned time and time again. We need some sort of memory help to tie these facts down.

Most people cannot tell you which is the port and which is the starboard side of a boat. Perhaps you have learned this and forgotten it repeatedly. Here is a simple way by which you can fix this fact indelibly in mind.

P-O-R-T is a word of four letters. So is the word L-E-F-T.

Again, *port* wine is *red*. So is the *port* light.

Weak Memory Strengthened

The weakest memory can be strengthened by methods just as natural and simple as these.

It all depends upon what sort of memory you have. If yours is strong enough to remember by merely *remembering*—well and good. But you will find, as you grow older, that the brain cells become less plastic—that brain paths form less easily. The slight impressions that served when you were younger will no longer suffice. You will need stronger means.

Steadily Improve Your Mind's Eye

Some minds need more coaching than others. All that the ordinary memory needs to operate better is to grasp the principle of visualization. Others require additional help, some of which is outlined in this lesson.

As we go forward, do not lose sight of this fact. It is just as important to improve your *mind's eye* as it is to learn the word lists.

Important Work Already Done

Although you have learned but fifty words in the first lesson, this work is of more importance than you realize. If you have done it conscientiously and well, you are now spinning along the highway of success to a far better memory than you ever had before.

These picture words, with some additional ones in this lesson, will not only give your imagination the exercise it needs but will also be of practical use to you.

Value of the New Words to Come

In this list there are one hundred words, including the first fifty. To those of you who are interested in remembering numbers—and this should include every one who desires to improve his memory—I suggest learning the new words in the same manner as you have learned the others.

This list is formed in accordance with a figure code that I will explain in Lesson Five.

These one hundred words are valuable in other ways, too. Take my advice, and visualize these word-pictures so that they will never be erased from your mind.

Before going further, recall your words from HAT to LACE, and backward from LACE to HAT.

The Fifty New Words

To LACE we will add the word LIGHT. See the LACE decorating an electric LIGHT.

Lesson Two

Make deep, strong impressions, and continue to introduce motion into your pictures. Later your memory will retain pictures that are not unusual.

Mental Cartooning Soon Becomes Automatic

Now picture LIGHT and LION.

The LIGHT is shining in the LION'S eyes and blinding him. He is moving about restlessly to avoid the LIGHT.

As explained in Lesson One, it is not necessary to follow my pictures. It is far better for you to form your own picture combinations.

Now see LION and LIME.

Some one has thrown LIME at the LION. Picture his antics when he tastes the LIME.

Now visualize LIME and LAWYER.

See the LAWYER rubbing LIME from his shoes.

Next combine

LAWYER and LILY
LILY   "   LODGE
LODGE   "   LAKE
LAKE   "   LOAF
LOAF   "   LAP
LAP   "   CHEESE

Review every group of *mental pictures* forward and backward as before. If you have difficulty in recalling a picture quickly, it will be because you have not made proper use of the principles laid down.

You can overcome this by making your visual picture clearer, or by strengthening it through further exaggeration and more motion.

Another Ten-Word Series

Make every picture as strong and as vivid as possible; retain it before your *mind's eye* a moment; then dismiss it while forming the next picture.

Picture **Cheese** and **Sheet**
Sheet " **Chain**
Chain " **Jam**
Jam " **Chair**
Chair " **Jail**
Jail " **Judge**
Judge " **Check**
Check " **Chief**
Chief " **Ship**
Ship " **Goose**

Try to form this next series of ten more quickly.

Goose and **Kite**
Kite " **Can**
Can " **Comb**
Comb " **Car**
Car " **Coal**
Coal " **Cage**
Cage " **Cake**
Cake " **Cuff**
Cuff " **Cab**
Cab " **Vase**

This Completes the List

Here is the final series of twenty words. See if you can impress the pictures they suggest on your mind in seven minutes or less. Accomplish this in five minutes, forming pictures that you can recall, and you will do well.

Vase and **Foot** | **Fan** and **Foam**
Foot " **Fan** | **Foam** " **Fire**

LESSON TWO 41

Fire and File	Piano and Bomb
File " Fish	Bomb " Bear
Fish " Fig	Bear " Bell
Fig " Fife	Bell " Bush
Fife " Fob	Bush " Bag
Fob " Bus	Bag " Beef
Bus " Boat	Beef " Pipe
Boat " Piano	Pipe " Daisies

First combine VASE and FOOT.

Then proceed through this series, ending with DAISIES, which completes the list.

After having mastered this last list of words, review the pictures from LACE to DAISIES, forward and backward.

Good Practice Methods

An excellent method for impressing your one hundred words will be to review them in groups of ten, selecting words here and there, and running through them.

For example, begin with WINDOW and review to MOOSE. Then RAT to LACE. Next TIDE to NOSE.

In the same way begin with the first word of every series of ten. The list is printed in series of ten words each to help you in this practice.

Your Code Words
First Fifty

Hat	Shoe	Tide	Dish	Window
Hen	Cow	Tin	Dog	Nun
Ham	Hive	Team	Dove	Gnome
Hare	Ape	Tire	Tub	Snare
Hill	Woods	Hotel	Nose	Nail

Hinge	Mud	Match	Rat	Roach
Ink	Moon	Hammock	Rain	Rake
Knife	Mummy	Muff	Ram	Roof
Knob	Hammer	Mop	Warrior	Rope
Moose	Mule	Rose	Rail	Lace

Your Code Words
Second Fifty

Light	Sheet	Kite	Foot	Boat
Lion	Chain	Can	Fan	Piano
Lime	Jam	Comb	Foam	Bomb
Lawyer	Chair	Car	Fire	Bear
Lily	Jail	Coal	File	Bell
Lodge	Judge	Cage	Fish	Bush
Lake	Check	Cake	Fig	Bag
Loaf	Chief	Cuff	Fife	Beef
Lap	Ship	Cab	Fob	Pipe
Cheese	Goose	Vase	Bus	Daisies

Make Practice Healthful and Interesting

Reviewing these mental pictures has proved a welcome relief from business to many students. The tense mind needs the complete relaxation afforded by a few moments devoted to visualization.

Open the window. Breathe deeply and often. Fill your lungs with fresh air. *Make a game out of your practice.*

Give your list to a second person. Tell him to select any word at random and you will name the word on either side of it. For example—if he mentions KNIFE you will know that INK comes before, and KNOB after it.

This you can do readily. Yet your friend, not in the secret, will be mystified and puzzled at the ease with which you do this. But do not explain how you do it. You can have more fun by not telling.

A Semi-Summary

Read this carefully. It contains in a nutshell what we have gone over.

1—You are eager to better your memory.
2—Everybody needs a memory file and index.
3—Here is one—not only easily learned—but logical and natural.
4—Learn to make these word-pictures quickly.
5—A one-hundred-word list of pictures—fifty of Lesson One and fifty new ones.
6—A knowledge of this one-hundred-word list is important. Attain it—and your progress is assured.
7—Strong *imagination, concentration,* and *clear thinking* make you master of any situation.

Real Concentration

In going over your mental pictures from HAT to DAISIES your mind is entirely occupied. It holds no other thoughts, because the mind can handle only one thought at a time. You are concentrating your entire attention, and this routine trains your concentrative powers for other things as well.

The review of this list at night has enabled many of my students to overcome insomnia.

It is just enough of a task to take the mind away from thoughts of business, or to prevent worry.

The Code Is of Great Value

These code words once learned will be no more of a burden to your mind than the A B C's. They are just as important in many ways as your alphabet.

My experience with thousands of business executives and professional men has proved that the student who follows instructions implicitly secures the best results.

Follow Instructions

You may think that some of this drill is superfluous. But I can assure you that the improvement you desire is dependent upon a thorough familiarity with the exercises in Lessons One and Two.

Just follow instructions.

A Big Reason Why

There are definite uses for these lists in memory training.

A certain amount of effort is needed to fix these words in the mind. This very effort is of the greatest value to you:

1—It creates a strong imagination.
2—It makes you the master of your mind; that is, it gives *concentration*.
3—It increases your reasoning powers, which is another way of saying you think more clearly.
4—Recalling your mind-pictures affords mental relaxation and, when necessary, takes your thoughts away from troublesome subjects.

To Forget

We can often reduce the acuteness of bitter thoughts that we should like to forget by visualization of pleasant pictures.

To forget—think constantly of something else.

The Mental Filing Code

The practice with your word-lists has prepared you for the next step. You are now ready to march boldly away, and to go to many definite places in Memoryland.

When you step into a hotel and hand your hat to the

boy in the checkroom you know you will get it when you call for it. It is not tossed into a corner, but hung on a numbered hook. The boy is systematic in his work.

You can do the same thing with a thought. Put it on a hook—a mental hook; file it in a mental pigeonhole. In other words, you associate the thought with one of your code words. This plan will now be explained.

Use of the One Hundred Words to Fix Ideas Permanently

The code words—HAT to DAISIES—will now serve as a series of mental *pigeonholes* in which you can store, for instant use, ideas, facts and other things difficult to remember.

Ideas come to us frequently at moments when we are busy with other thoughts. The ideas may be so clear that we feel sure we shall recall them later. Then, when we wish to refer to them, they have vanished.

Many good ideas are lost in this way. They may come to us at night, during an auto trip, while playing golf, or at other times when it is inconvenient or impossible for us to make written notes.

Good Ideas Retained

Here is where our Mental Filing Code is of extreme value. If you prevent an occasional good idea from being lost, or if you get a mental grasp on some important engagement that you might otherwise miss, you will be repaid richly for the time devoted to this subject.

But you will be repaid in many other ways. *Things learned in an interesting way are always retained best.* This is one of the great factors in these memory lessons.

Practical Use of Mental Pigeonholes

This plan is so simple, yet so important to you in many ways, that I want you to grasp it clearly. I can illustrate the application of the mental pigeonholes best by having you put them into immediate use and file away ten grocery items.

For All Purposes

Bear in mind that this method enables you to remember the merest trifle and the most important things with equal certainty.

1—The first article is *butter*. Instead of merely thinking of butter, you must picture it. But picturing it alone is not sufficient. There may be nothing later on to recall to you this picture of butter.

You must—as we shall express it from now on—file it in the first pigeonhole of your mental filing cabinet.

Using the First Ten Code Words

Our old friend HAT—the picture you learned first—is to be your first pigeonhole.

To make sure you will recall butter when necessary, merely form a picture of HAT and butter.

See the HAT and into it drop a large brick of butter. See the butter fall into the HAT.

We have now bound together the two objects, HAT and butter, in a new mental picture.

2—Your next grocery item is *sugar*. File this in your second pigeonhole, which is HEN. See the HEN picking and clawing a hole in a bag of sugar.

3—*Toothpicks* is next on the list. The third pigeonhole is HAM. Stick a lot of toothpicks into a HAM.

LESSON TWO

You can now proceed in the same manner with the following items:

4—Bread. File this in the next pigeonhole, which is HARE. Make a clear picture combining HARE and bread.

5—Soap. File this in its proper place. The pigeonhole is, of course, HILL. See the bar of soap balanced on the top of the HILL or sliding down its slope.

6—Cocoa. The pigeonhole is SHOE. Form a picture of a SHOE and a can of cocoa.

7—Macaroni. File this in the COW pigeonhole in a clear picture.

8—Raisins. Mentally store this in the HIVE pigeonhole.

9—Can of corn. File this with the next pigeonhole—the APE.

10—Oranges. Picture these in the WOODS.

You have now formed a series of mental pictures similar to the accompanying illustrations:

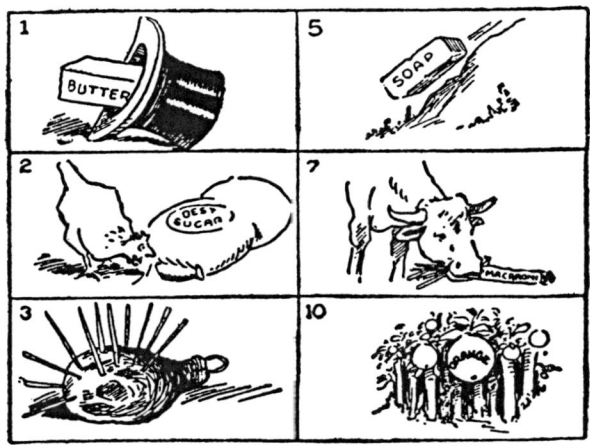

Now—Remember

Go back to your first pigeonhole—the HAT.
1—Recall the picture of the article you put in the HAT. It was *butter*.
2—HEN will recall the *sugar*.
3—HAM brings back the picture of the *Toothpicks*.
4—HARE reminds you of *bread*.
5—HILL makes you think of *soap*.
6—SHOE suggests the *cocoa*.
7—COW suggests *macaroni*.
8—HIVE recalls *raisins*.
9—APE reminds you of *corn*.
10—WOODS enables you to remember *oranges*.

You see now how familiarity with your Code Words makes it easy for your mind to go from one pigeonhole to the next and in this way recall all your errands.

Any Idea Can Be Thus Filed

Any idea can be filed by making a combination picture of the pigeonhole code-word and the idea you desire to keep in mind. Some pictures combine more naturally than others, but your previous training will make it easily possible for you to form the combinations.

As I have been careful to point out to you, it is essential to develop a smoothly running imagination so that you can form the unusual picture-combinations quickly.

Remembering Ten Errands

File the following errands mentally by placing them in your next series of Picture-Pigeonholes. *It is surprisingly easy to remember things when you proceed systematically.*

Lesson Two

Pigeonhole	Errand
TIDE	Buy a trunk
TIN	See the Printer
TEAM	Dentist Appointment
TIRE	Buy stamps
HOTEL	Pay light bill
DISH	Buy gloves
DOG	Reserve berth
DOVE	Buy book
TUB	Order flowers
NOSE	Druggist

Associate in picture form the pigeonhole and the item that is to be remembered. Form a picture that will recall the errand, the place, or the thing you wish to do.

You are putting every one of these items, or errands, away in a definite mental location. The pigeonholes will then recall your errands, as:

> TIDE recalls *buy a trunk.*
> TIN suggests *printer.*
> TEAM reminds you of *dentist.*
> TIRE brings back *stamps.*
> HOTEL will recall *light bill.*
> DISH brings up *gloves.*
> DOG is to *reserve berth.*
> DOVE recalls the *book.*
> TUB suggests order *flowers.*
> NOSE reminds you of *druggist.*

Having placed these associations in mind, review the pictures once or twice. If you have trouble in recalling the thoughts filed in one or more of the pigeonholes, you will find that you did not make the picture definite enough.

In such cases, *make more of an impression by forming a larger, or more unusual picture, or by making the objects more animated.*

To Clear the Records

The question is asked frequently whether the butter will not persist in being associated with the HAT, and the HEN with the sugar. The fear is expressed that this will interfere with the filing of other items in these pigeonholes.

It is quite true that in the beginning the butter and the HAT are going to stick together for a while, as well as the HEN and the sugar or the HAM and the toothpicks. This is due, however, to the fact that the method is a new one for you and that you are making a stronger effort, and reviewing these first pictures many times.

After you have practiced with your mental pigeonholes a few more times these pictures that you no longer wish to use will pass away quickly—*the slate wipes itself clean.*

Even if the butter persists in sticking with the HAT for a while, this does not interfere with using the HAT for other purposes at the same time.

Two More Practice Lists

For example, here are two additional practice lists—the *auto list* and the *day's schedule*. Many students find it easy to file lists like these in the same series of pigeonholes, one shortly after the other, and without confusion:

Auto List	*Day's Schedule*
1—Batteries.	1—Pay life insurance.
2—Clutch.	2—Telephone doctor.
3—Grease.	3—Go to bank.
4—Tubes.	4—Order stationery.

LESSON TWO 51

    Auto List   *Day's Schedule*
5—Basket.   5—Telephone White.
6—Horn.   6—Scissors sharpened.
7—Spark plug.   7—Buy golf balls.
8—Gloves.   8—Select furniture
9—Robe.   9—Buy wedding present.
10—Wrench.   10—See tailor.

File away the auto list by associating b a t t e r i e s with HAT, c l u t c h wit h HEN, and g r e a s e with HAM.

In the same way continue through the list. W r e n c h, —the last item—will be pictured with WOODS.

Recall these items, in regular order, then select any code word and see if you can recall the associated object.

Later in the day proceed in the same way with the day's schedule, filing the items with your first ten code words. Picture l i f e i n s u r a n c e and HAT, d o c t o r with HEN, and so on.

Recall Your Associations

Then recall them. You will find that while the two lists may conflict at times, it is entirely practical to carry them in mind without serious confusion.

If more than ten items are to be filed at one time, begin with HAT and in regular order, use as many code words as necessary.

Let us suppose you are through with one list and wish to file away a new list in the same pigeonholes you have recently used, say HAT to WOODS.

Before starting on the new list that you plan to file, it is well to run over your pigeonholes a few times—thus: HAT, HEN, HAM, HARE, HILL, SHOE, COW, HIVE, APE, WOODS. By doing this you will weaken the impression of the previous list, and your code words will be ready for the new associations.

Use Your Own Lists

Please understand that these lists are for practice only. But the practice is valuable. It is necessary, at first, to take simple things, such as, perhaps, you never have to bother with, in order to become familiar with the process.

It is not intended that you should retain these lists for any length of time. You are to file them away for temporary use only. *If you have any lists of your own, practice on them*—either your own list of errands and engagements, or any list that you may have occasion to remember.

Thirty Pigeonholes for Mental Filing

The words HAT to DAISIES furnish you with one hundred mental pigeonholes. For most practical purposes the first twenty, or perhaps thirty, are sufficient. Therefore, I urge you, to pay careful attention to the words from HAT to MOOSE. Take time to learn and to review them thoroughly.

Add This Method to Your Own

It is not my intention to develop an artificial or mechanical memory for you.

I do not recommend that you discard as worthless the making of memoranda, nor do I wish you to give up any helpful method of remembering that you may have worked out for yourself. But I do wish you to add to those methods the means I have suggested.

A Sure Method

Many times during the day, or, perhaps, more often at night, ideas may come to you that you wish to nail down tight. Perhaps you find it impossible to write them down at the time, and so they are forgotten.

Now I have shown you how to visualize the idea and lash it, either temporarily or permanently, to the code word so that you can recall it at will, even though you have no written memoranda.

Hat Our Daily Reminder

Here is a valuable suggestion for remembering the various things you may wish to do during the day.

One of my students had no difficulty in making and filing mental pictures. But he needed something definite to remind him to do things before he started for home.

I suggested that he make the hat he wore remind him of his code words. Every time he put on or took off his hat it made him think of HAT, HEN, HAM.

In this manner, if he had anything filed away, he was sure to recall it. He put this idea into practice with excellent results.

You can use the same method to good advantage, and go through your code list, checking off the things as you do them.

Some people make written memoranda and then forget them. Your HAT reminder will help you if you are one of those who depend upon the memorandum pad.

To Pigeonhole Temporarily or Permanently

The question is often asked by students, when they first come to this idea of pigeonholing ideas, "How should I handle those ideas that I wish to pigeonhole temporarily, such as the list of errands, in comparison with those I wish to remember permanently, such as the talking points of a selling proposition?"

For permanent retention, every picture must be reviewed a number of times. Every time the picture is revisualized the impression upon the brain is deepened.

For temporary use, one or two reviews will be sufficient.

For the list of errands, or any temporary things, do not make the mistake of reviewing frequently the visual impressions. Just see the pictures clearly a few times. Then you will have the code word free and clear tomorrow for an *entirely different* list of temporary things.

Lasting Impressions

For permanent record it is necessary that our *mind's-eye* pictures be reviewed from time to time.

Recall them occasionally and they will remain with you.

The mental file and code is useful in business, professional, or social life. It is used by public speakers, sales managers, storekeepers, and by a host of other people who must remember quickly and correctly.

Note This Important Fact

An unlimited number of ideas can be stored permanently in every one of your pigeonholes.

You can file many things permanently with every code word and there will be no confusion. These ideas will not conflict with one another. Neither will they interfere with other ideas that you may file temporarily.

Practical Applications

The mental pigeonholes can be used in every business or profession. Again let me make it clear that I do not

LESSON TWO 55

expect the student, who is at times flooded with details, to store them all away mentally. There are times when information, business engagements, and many details may swamp you. Under such circumstances it may be advisable to make a written list of these things.

Memory Training Develops Will Power

But keep this thought in mind: Mental filing practiced regularly is a great mind stimulant. It develops *Will Power.*

The mind does not take kindly to restraint. It tries to follow the path of least resistance—to take the easiest way. Make it obey your commands.

Form Mental Pictures on every occasion and you will acquire a firmness and ability to control the source of your greatest power.

Understand clearly that the simple exercises laid down in these lessons accomplish much more for you than a better memory—they strengthen your mind.

If you have a strong, creative mind—an imagination that may be used at will, the power of concentration, the power of logical reason and an accurate memory, you are at all times Master of the Situation.

Exercises That Work Wonders for You

The value of Lessons One and Two cannot be overestimated. Read them carefully and often. Follow every exercise as outlined.

By all means practice Mental Pigeonholing with the practice lists on page 16 as well as with lists of your own.

You can make this practice entertaining as well as

beneficial. Show others how easily you can retain and recall any simple lists which they may give you.

Remember always that this practice is giving that mental control and will power which is so necessary for success in any field.

> *You cannot run away from a weakness; you must sometime fight it out or perish, and if that be so why not now and where you stand.*
> —Robert Louis Stevenson.

Sales Talks

A man cannot refer to notes when he is making a sales talk. He must depend upon his memory. A salesman frequently thinks of excellent arguments after he has left his "prospect."

In many lines of business the salesman must be fully conversant with sales points and specifications. Inability to learn these has retarded many a man's progress.

The man who applies the principles in these lessons can learn quickly sales points and information, which would otherwise overwhelm him.

Increase Your Earning Power

Many of my students have increased their ability, and their earning capacity, by applying this method of mental pigeonholing.

If you need to learn a sales talk, every subject should represent a definite picture, and must be associated with a code word. These are permanent impressions, and they should be recalled repeatedly to be sure they are well fixed in mind.

If you need information of this kind, and have been handicapped in the past because you could not fix it in mind, learn your HAT, HEN, HAM list of words. Then practice pigeonholing and recalling the points you wish to retain. This method offers a wonderful opportunity for the man with a faulty memory.

If you are thoroughly familiar with part of a talk there is no need to use your pigeonholes for that section of it. But you can always be sure of new topics by associating them with the code words.

Certainty Instead of Uncertainty

Many men present their sales talk in a hit-and-miss way, never following the same presentation twice. *There is always one best arrangement for most propositions.* A little thought will outline the most logical and effective way. Fix this arrangement in mind by linking the first point with HAT, the second with HEN, and so on.

A good memory is priceless in business.

One student made quick advance after completing the lessons. He told me he had never taken the time previously to do any planning. Now he uses a few minutes formerly spent in rushing around, and arranges his thoughts, duties and calls systematically. He then mentally pigeonholes them, and, as a result, he has practically doubled his capacity.

Remembering Wants

It is often convenient and at times necessary to carry in mind items that should be ordered. When the number is limited the pigeonhole plan can be used. Later the items may be listed in the want book.

The pigeonholes are also convenient at times for receiving orders when conditions render it impossible to write them.

Public Speaking

A brief outline will show how the mental pigeonholes will serve the public speaker, lawyer, minister, teacher, business or professional man.

Let me again emphasize this important fact:

This method of mental pigeonholing is not designed to take the place of any means you have used successfully heretofore.

If you can get along without the necessity of pigeonholing, by all means do so. But if you have trouble in remembering the things you wish to do, or say, then you are making a great mistake if you neglect this method.

A better impression is always made by the speaker who dispenses with notes. Given some time for preparation, there is little need for written memoranda. They can be held in reserve for reference if needed.

This is especially advisable for the man who has depended upon notes in the past, and is now breaking himself of this habit.

Notes for a Five-Minute Talk

Here are seven points of a brief talk on a commercial product. They are as difficult to picture as any that we meet ordinarily.

1—Economical.   3—Convenient.   6—Service.
2—Quick.   4—Well advertised.   7—Guaranteed.
   5—Interchangeable.

Suggestions

Following are suggestions for the visual association of every topic, and for the pigeonhole:

1—HAT—Economical.
   A picture of some one carefully brushing, cleaning or repairing an old HAT to avoid the necessity of buying a new one—*economical*.
2—HEN—Quick.
   See a HEN running. Recalling this picture a few times will impress the idea of *quick*.
3—HAM—Convenient.
   Picture of a hungry man with a HAM finding it *convenient* to cut off a slice.
4—HARE—Well advertised.
   See a HARE sitting up and carefully perusing a large billboard or advertisement—*well advertised*.
5—HILL—Interchangeable.
   See a party of tourists carefully changing positions on a steep HILL or mountain trail—*interchangeable*.
6—SHOE—Service.
   Picture a SHOE that has given extra good *service*.
7—COW—Guaranteed.
   Picture a food inspector pasting a *guaranteed* label on a COW.

No Danger of Confusion

If you will impress your pictures by recalling them a sufficient number of times, interruptions, questions, or new thoughts will not make you lose the thread of your remarks.

When you are through talking about the convenient feature that is associated with HAM, you know your next pigeonhole is HARE. This brings to mind the picture of the advertisement, suggesting your next theme: *well advertised*.

How to Remember Stories

People usually forget stories as quickly as they hear them. The stories were clear and impressive when heard, and you believed that you would always remember a few of the best ones. Yet in a day or two you found it impossible to recall them.

The code words will enable you always to keep in mind a goodly number of stories. There is always a feature of every story that can be associated with a code word.

By using this plan you can readily file away fifteen or twenty anecdotes. Recall every association a few times, and you will have them all ready for use when needed.

Code Words for Stories

When you have occasion to use stories, a review of your code words will give instant access to the several anecdotes, from which you can make your selection. In this lesson we shall not consider the actual memorizing of the story. If you have difficulty in this respect you will find Lesson Four helpful.

Use Your Code Words

We shall now see how the point, or the subject of the story, can be kept in mind—most of us have no difficulty in telling the story if we can recall the subject.

Here are a few good stories selected at random to illustrate the principle by which they can be kept in mind, and recalled when needed.

Lesson Four contains additional aid on the subject of public speaking.

A Wonderful Gift

"Who-all sick up to yo' house, Mis' Smif?" asked George Washington Jones.

"It's mah brudder 'Lige," replied Mrs. Smith.

"What's he done got de mattah wif him?"

"Dey cain't tell. He eats an' he sleeps all right, an' he stays out in de veranda in de sun all day, but he cain't do no wuhk at all."

"He cain't wuhk?"

"Not a bit."

Mr. Jones raised his eyes to heaven. "Law, Mis' Smif, dat ain't no disease what yo' brudder's got. Dat air am a gift."

The point of the first story is *gift*. Associate gift and HAT by forming a picture of some one making you a gift of a hat. See the hat as it is presented to you and see yourself try it on, with a pleased smile. Later, your code word HAT will serve to recall the point of the story—*gift*.

No Free Ads for Stradivarius

A violinist was bitterly disappointed with the account of his recital printed in the paper of a small town.

"I told your man three or four times," complained the musician to the owner of the paper, "that the instrument I used was a genuine Stradivarius, and in his story there was not a word about it, not a word."

Whereupon the owner said with a laugh:

"That is as it should be. When Mr. Stradivarius gets his fiddles advertised in my paper under ten cents a line, you come around and let me know."

The foregoing story can be filed away by forming a mental picture of a HEN playing a *violin—a Stradivarius*.

Considerable Effort

A country man drifted into a little village drug store in Georgia and asked for a nickel's worth of Eucalyptus. The clerk proceeded to wrap it up and, on handing it to the customer, was told to "charge it." "What name?" said the clerk. "Honeyfunckel," said the customer. Whereupon the clerk remarked, "Take it—I wouldn't write Eucalyptus and Honeyfunckel for a nickel."

The above anecdote may be associated with HAM by forming an association of a HAM covered with *Eucalyptus*.

Pleasant Neighbors

Uncle Josh—Here's a letter from Nephew Harry that's gone to Africa, and says that within twenty rods of his house there's a family of laughing hyenas.

His Wife—"Well, I am glad he's got pleasant neighbors, anyway—that's something."

This story can be kept in mind by forming a picture of a HARE being chased by a *family of laughing hyenas*.

Views of His Own

Ticket Agent—"Here are some post-card views along our railroad line. Would you like them?"

Cynical Patron—"Thanks, no. Since I have gone over the line I have views of my own on it."

This brisk bit of repartee can be associated with HILL by picturing yourself viewing a railroad from the top of a HILL, or with a camera taking *views of your own*.

These five illustrations show the way in which stories can be linked with any code word. By following this plan when you hear stories you can recall many of them later.

Constant use of Imagination, Visualization, and Association will work wonders for your memory.

Bits of Wisdom

The following epigrams can be kept in mind by linking each one with a code word.

The trouble with the average memory is the inability to bring these thoughts back when they are wanted.

The code words enable you to carry in mind a large number of helpful suggestions. These must be recalled from time to time. Before long these and similar thoughts will become as familiar to you as the alphabet.

System and Regularity Work Wonders

Learn one of the following every day. Recall it frequently. Every day review the previous thoughts and at the end of twenty days you will have mastered twenty helpful suggestions.

Lesson Two

Great results follow systematic effort. You can see readily that a few minutes every day, applied properly, will soon enrich your mental storehouse.

Make the most of your time. The minutes that are lost can never be regained.

Learn One Bit Every Day

1—"All men are born equal—but that is where the equality ends."
2—"The man who is without an idea has generally the greatest idea of himself."
3—"In the orchard of Opportunity it is better to pick the fruit than to wait for it to fall."
4—"It is better to say a good word about a bad fellow than a bad word about a good fellow."
5—"Today is the tomorrow that you were worrying about yesterday—and it didn't happen."
6—"When we sigh about our trouble
It grows double—every day.
When we laugh about a trouble
It's a bubble—blown away."
7—"Smile a while—
And while you smile, another smiles,
And soon there's miles and miles of smiles,
And life's worth while, because you smile."
8—"It's not the load, but thinking about it that makes you tired."
9—"When you can find nothing to do, your case is desperate."
10—"When you find the best way, abolish all others."
11—"A little of the smiling bluff
Oft proves to be the winning stuff.
A little laugh or honest grin
Has pulled full many a prospect in."
12—"It is not enough to know, we must also apply; it is not enough to will, we must also do."
13—"There's a vast difference between having a carload of miscellaneous facts sloshing around loose in your head and getting all mixed up in transit, and carrying the same assortment properly boxed and crated for convenient handling and immediate delivery."
14—"He that can take rest is greater than he that can take cities."
15—"He that speaks must is much mistaken."
16—"To be humble to superiors is duty; to equals, courtesy; to inferiors, nobleness."

17—"Breathe deeply, eat slowly, be cheerful and go to sleep with strong, healthy thoughts."
18—"One today is worth two tomorrows."
19—" 'Tis easier to suppress the first desire than to satisfy all that follow it."
20—"The eye of the master will do more work than both his hands."

Other Applications

I wish to impress upon you that there are many other ways in which these principles can be applied effectively. A little ingenuity and practice will make it easy, and will help you pleasantly over many a difficult road. A test every day, similar to the grocery list, stimulates mental activity.

Mental filing, practiced regularly, brings increased memory power that later enables you to remember details without the use of the code words.

A FINAL SUMMARY

1—Here is a memory file in which to store ideas.
2—The basis of this mental file is one hundred word-pictures.
3—For practical use it is necessary to make mental pictures quickly.
4—Practice toward this end will develop strong imagination, concentration, and clear thinking—a triangle of brain power that must win recognition for its possessor.
5—Knowing this code of word-pictures, we have one hundred pigeonholes in which ideas we wish to remember can be stored for either temporary or permanent use.
6—A quick grasp of at least thirty code words is essential.
7—Items to be remembered should be visualized with the code words in regular order.
8—To recall such lists, start with the first code word and go through the series of visualized pictures.
9—For temporary use the visual impressions should be dismissed as soon as their need is over. For permanent retention, make deep, strong impressions and review them regularly.
10—Practical applications—sales talks, public speaking and stories.

PRACTICE CHART 2

Recall your picture associations for the following code words. To the left, write the word which precedes the code word—to the right, the word which follows the code word. Note example: *Fish* precedes *FIG*—*Fife* follows FIG.

Fish	Fig	*Fife*	_____	Fish	_____
_____	Car	_____	_____	Bomb	_____
_____	Bus	_____	_____	Jail	_____
_____	Can	_____	_____	Fife	_____
_____	Fob	_____	_____	Bush	_____
_____	Cab	_____	_____	Cake	_____
_____	Fan	_____	_____	Vase	_____
_____	Lap	_____	_____	Fire	_____
_____	Bag	_____	_____	Ship	_____
_____	Jam	_____	_____	Lake	_____
_____	Cuff	_____	_____	File	_____
_____	Bell	_____	_____	Foot	_____
_____	Lime	_____	_____	Chain	_____
_____	Bear	_____	_____	Goose	_____
_____	Lily	_____	_____	Judge	_____
_____	Kite	_____	_____	Sheet	_____
_____	Coal	_____	_____	Light	_____
_____	Lion	_____	_____	Chair	_____
_____	Boat	_____	_____	Lodge	_____
_____	Comb	_____	_____	Chief	_____
_____	Beef	_____	_____	Piano	_____
_____	Foam	_____	_____	Check	_____
_____	Cage	_____	_____	Cheese	_____
_____	Loaf	_____	_____	Lawyer	_____

PRACTICE CHART 3

Daily tests for exercise. Form picture associations between the following words and your code words as indicated:

1st Day HAT to WOODS:		2nd Day TIDE to NOSE:	
Ice	Navy	Coffee	Wire
Desk	Steam	Ledger	Stone
Pencil	Board	Rubber	Euchre
Watch	Flower	Preacher	Postage
Camera	Engine	Shipment	General
3rd Day WINDOW to MOOSE:		4th Day HAT to WOODS:	
Stove	Frog	Pick	Salt
Badge	Bank	Ferry	Paddle
Huron	Violin	Toast	Cashier
Turkey	Ribbon	Whale	St. Louis
Tractor	Baltimore	Honey	Michigan
5th Day TIDE to NOSE:		6th Day WINDOW to MOOSE:	
Bark	Clerk	Pin	Grant
China	Garage	Sister	Illinois
Quail	Mexico	Bubble	Forgive
Indiana	Invoice	Buckeye	Revolution
Telegram	C. O. D.	Mackenzie	Treacherous

See how quickly you can form and how correctly you can recall your pictures.

These exercises quicken your visualizing and associative power.

Do not make any attempt to store these pictures for permanent record. They are intended for exercise only. Continue taking tests similar to these.

LESSON THREE

How to Remember Names and Faces

Every One Can Acquire This Ability

Faces and names are the doorplates and doorknobs of business and social success.

Until we can read the one and grasp the other we are shut off from intimate intercourse with the very people it is essential we should meet, greet, and know familiarly.

Doubtless you are acquainted with people who seem to have a gift of remembering the names and faces of those they meet. Perhaps you have fallen into the common error of believing this ability is always a gift—a natural accomplishment. If so, you are mistaken, and I shall give you, in the following lesson, some valuable suggestions on the matter of remembering names and faces, so that you will be able to remember as well as your friends, and very much better.

This prediction is based on my own experience. I began business life with an unusually poor ability to remember names and faces. I set about overcoming this handicap with the result that when introduced to fifty or a hundred strangers at a business or social meeting I can call almost every person by name.

Easy and Practical

Many young people have exceptionally retentive memories, but, as they grow older, this natural ability leaves them, and they feel alarmed over their loss of mental power. This failing is easily corrected by following the simple, practical principles by which I improved my own memory.

However, do not expect a miracle to happen. You have neglected remembering names so long that you cannot now recall them at will. You will have to strive for gradual improvement. *If you will couple the desire to remember names with my suggestions, a vast improvement can be made quickly.* You know that anything worth having is worth striving for.

When you forget a name, the memory is not at fault. It is due to failure on your part to observe the principles by which the name could have been *retained.* You do not expect a stamp to stick without moistening it. Neither will a name stick without some effort on your part to help the memory.

Your ability to recall the face proves that the application of the right methods should enable you to retain the name.

The General Rules

If you wish to make quick progress you must be familiar with the previous lessons and observe the following principles:

I—*You must pay attention.* Be sure you hear the name correctly. If you are not certain about it, ask to have it repeated. You cannot remember the name if you do not *hear* it clearly.

II—*You must observe closely the appearance of the person whom you are meeting.*

LESSON THREE   71

III—*You must make some association of the name and the appearance of the person.*

These are cardinal principles and should always be borne in mind when you are introduced to strangers.

Attention

You have discovered by observing the principles of *Visualization, Imagination,* and *Association,* and by the review of your words in Lessons One and Two, that every repetition makes it easier for you to see the pictures you have created in your *mind's eye.* This was done by paying close *attention* to every word.

You first heard the word—so you had a sound impression upon the memory. Through the use of *imagination* you created the object that the word represented. Then, by the use of *visualization,* you saw it in your *mind's eye.* Every one of the hundred words suggested a distinct picture.

Now if you will pay attention and use your *imagination,* you will meet many people whose names will also suggest something that you can grasp and picture.

Endeavor to make the name you hear really represent some distinct object or idea in addition to the mere sound as you store it in your memory. For instance:

1—*Baer* can be imagined and seen in
              the *mind's eye* as a b e a r .

2—*Hogg* can be imagined and seen in
              the *mind's eye* as a h o g .

3—*Lyon* can be imagined and seen in the *mind's eye* as a l i o n.

4—*Rhoades* can be imagined and seen in the *mind's eye* as a r o a d.

5—*Stohne* can be imagined and seen in the *mind's eye* as a s t o n e.

You will meet with many names that do not lend themselves to visualization as readily as the foregoing, which are selected because of their simplicity to illustrate the method. But a little practice will make many difficult names easy to remember.

Observation

The average person does not retain in the memory over forty per cent of the things he hears or sees, because he is deficient in the power of observation.

To develop this power you must train yourself to see more closely than has been your habit. You must note if the stranger whom you meet is tall or short, thin or stout, dark or fair, weak or strong. Note the color of the eyes, eyebrows, face, and hair. See the shape of the head, mouth, chin, nose, ears, and so on.

Mere Looking Is Not Observation

In other words, SEE. Merely *looking at* the person and not recording a distinct impression is not observing.

Begin to take notice of these things among your friends and new acquaintances. You will usually observe something about the appearance of the individual that will enable you to make a *mind's eye* picture that can be linked with the name.

The following are a few of many people I have met whose appearance gave a distinct clue to the name. Although instances such as these are not general yet they are far more common than the unobservant person would believe.

    Mr. *Baldwin* was bald, so the suggestion of b a l d o n e was formed.

    Mr. *Eyster* had a fixed look in his eyes, reminding me of e y e s t a r e .

    Mr. *Lipps* had large thick lips, suggesting l i p s .

    Mr. *Sharpe* had a pointed nose, suggesting s h a r p .

A Pleasant Pastime

A little application of this principle will give you much enjoyment and will soon become a pleasant pastime. *If you will combine your observation of faces with what you know of the character of the individual you will, in time, become a good judge of human nature.*

Most people say "I can't remember names, but I seldom forget a face."

This is not strange, for memory of the face is entirely a *visual* impression, which comes to you through the eye. You have learned that this is the *strongest* kind of impression. The name is registered through the ear—an auditory impression.

Use Your Mind's Eye

It is necessary to bring your *mind's eye* into action to make a visual impression of the *meaning* of the name.

If you read a story, or hear a speech, and the word *pike* is mentioned, you readily see the *pike* in your *mind's eye*.

When you meet a Mr. *Pike* probably no thought of the *pike* enters your mind. But the two words are identical and have the same meaning.

A name may convey more than one idea. *Pike* suggests a *turnpike,* a *pike*-pole, and a *pike*-fish.

Mr. *Pike,* pictured in your *mind's eye* as in the accompanying illustration, will be recalled easily. Try to see the face and the entire illustration as you look away from the page.

To be successful in remembering names you must

Lesson Three

cultivate the habit of noting the meaning, and of making your MIND'S EYE *register for you a picture of this meaning.*

Follow this plan whenever possible. *Convert the auditory impression you receive when you hear a name into a visual record, which is more lasting and more readily recalled.*

You will be pleased at the number of names that can be indelibly impressed in this manner.

Mr. Shepard is pictured here. Think of this as *shepherd* and form a *mind's-eye* picture. See how easily you will recall his name when the face appears later on.

MR. SHEPARD

Association

Association is the foundation of all memory. Without association of some kind there can be no memory. When a name recurs to you without effort on your part there has been association, although you may not realize it.

Understand this thoroughly:

Memory is based on several definite impressions recorded in the mind at the same time, and in such manner that the recall of one impression brings back the other. This is association.

Whenever one of two things that have been associated

in the mind recurs, it tends to recall the other. This is the very basis of memory.

This is why you remember a name that flashes into your mind, seemingly without effort, when you see the face.

Association of Face and Name

The visual impression of the face, and the sound of the name reached the mind at the same time and formed a definite association. The reappearance of the face revived its associated impression—the sound of the name.

Such association—the most simple and natural sort—is not sufficient for the recall of most names. You must strengthen your mental records in other ways.

The strongest bond you can form is to have an association between the face impression and some picture that the name suggests. See them together in your *mind's eye.*

There are other means by which the memory of names and faces can be strengthened. These I shall treat in the order of their relative importance. *Anything done toward associating the name with something familiar to you will be of aid.*

You will be able now, even without further instruction, to improve your ability to remember names and faces. If you will make use of the various suggestions in the succeeding pages the subject will become most interesting and helpful.

The following sketch illustrates some of the associations that may be formed when you meet a Mr. *Campbell.*

LESSON THREE 77

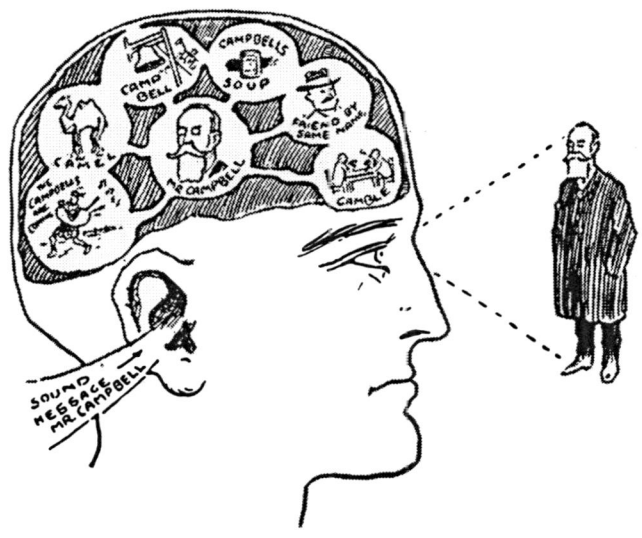

The Natural Method

As you exercise and train your memory you will find its power to retain information greatly increases. It may be possible soon for you to remember many names and faces in the *natural* way simply by seeing the face and hearing the name spoken. Very few people possess this natural ability.

For the present, when meeting strangers, you must follow my suggestions for remembering names.

Regular use of these methods will develop quickly the

habit of remembering names as well as faces. You will find much of interest in the subject, as all names originally had a meaning.

A large part of them can be ascribed to the occupation, residence, and virtues or imperfections of our ancestors. Others have derived their meaning from the names of birds, beasts, colors, location, seasons, or accidental circumstances that created a nickname that became a permanent family name.

The following poem, by James Smith, will give you an idea of many peculiarities found in the subject of names and faces:

>Men once were surnamed from their shape or estate
> (You all may from history worm it;)
>There was Lewis the Bulky, and Henry the Great,
> John Lackland, and Peter the Hermit.
>But now, when the doorplates of misters and dames
> Are read, each so constantly varies
>From the owner's trade, figure, and calling, surnames
> Seem given by the rule of contraries.
>
>Mr. *Box,* though provoked, never doubles his fist,
> Mr. *Burns,* in his grate, has no fuel;
>Mr. *Playfair* won't catch me at hazard or whist,
> Mr. *Coward* was winged in a duel.
>Mr. *Wise* is a dunce, Mr. *King* is a whig,
> Mr. *Coffin's* uncommonly sprightly,
>And huge Mr. *Little* broke down in a gig
> While driving fat Mrs. *Golightly.*
>
>Miss *Joy,* wretched maid, when she chose Mr. *Love,*
> Found nothing but sorrow await her;
>She now holds in wedlock, as true as a dove,
> That fondest of mates, Mr. *Hayter.*
>Mrs. *Drinkwater's* apt to indulge in a dram,
> Mrs. *Angel's* an abs'lute fury,
>And meek Mr. *Lyon* let fierce Mr. *Lamb*
> Tweak his nose in the lobby of Drury.

Lesson Three

Mr. *Child,* in a passion, knocked down Mr. *Rock,*
  Mr. *Stone* like an aspen leaf shivers;
Miss *Poole* used to dance, but she stands like a stock
  Ever since she became Mrs. *Rivers.*
Mr. *Swift* hobbles onward, no mortal knows how,
  He moves as though cords had entwined him;
Mr. *Metcalf* ran off, upon meeting a cow,
  With pale Mr. *Turnbull* behind him.

Mr. *Barker's* as mute as a fish in the sea,
  Mr. *Miles* never moves on a journey;
Mr. *Early* sits up till half after three,
  Mr. *Makepeace* was bred an attorney.
Mr. *Gardiner* can't tell a flower from a root,
  Mr. *Wilde* with timidity draws back,
Mr. *Ryder* performs all his journeys on foot,
  Mr. *Foote* all his journeys on horseback.

The sketches shown will also call your attention to names especially fitting, or most inappropriate.

Mr. Long Mr. Short Mr. Poor Mr. Rich Mr. Gladden Mr. Madden

Common Names Full of Meaning

It would be easy to mention many ordinary names that suggest clear cut *mind's eye* pictures. A few such names are presented here. As you read this list picture every object. You will find it possible to enlarge this list to an unlimited extent.

Stone	Bell	Cotton	Graves
Brooks	Hoe	Light	Thorn
Root	Forest	Starr	Water
Walker	River	Lake	Branch

Many of the names, which you hear frequently, have definite meanings. These can be impressed upon your mind by forming pictures of the objects suggested.

Follow this plan of picturing the meaning conveyed by a name, and you will at once improve your memory.

One of my students—a man prominent in civic life—thought it impossible for him to remember names. After his lesson on names, he met three strangers—Mr. Baer, Mr. Rohr, and Mr. Spencer. These names now meant something to him and were readily recalled.

Mr. B a e r suggested a grizzly *bear*.

Mr. R o h r a *roar*ing waterfall.

Mr. S p e n c e r the *Spencer*ian pen.

MR. FLOWER

The picture on this page is that of Mr. *Flower*. Form a *mind's-eye* image of a *flower* or *flour*. You will be asked to name him later.

Other Suggestive Names

Names are interesting and often amusing. A short time ago a football game was won by the kicking of Bill Boote. The newspaper writer said "There must be something in a name after all, since Bill Boote, the big lanky left halfback twice lived up to his name by booting the ball over the goal posts."

Another bright scribe comments on names as follows: "The Willys-Overland agent in Paris, Texas, named Briscoe Dodge Chandler, ought to go into partnership with A. Ford Carr, of Chicago."

Instances such as these are not at all unusual. Names seem to have no limit. They have been drawn from every conceivable source and are still coming.

Orchard and Farm

Here are a few examples:

Baldwin suggests *apple*.   Crawford suggests *peach*.
Hubbard   "   *squash*.   Murphy   "   *potato*.

Animals, Birds, Fish

We meet them daily—names like the following:

Fox	Wolf	Hogg
Bear'	Lyons	Martin
Partridge	Robbins	Wrenn
Salmon	Sturgeon	Herring

Colors, Fruits, Flowers, Metals

Brown	Berry	Rose	Gold
Gray	Apple	Astor	Silver
White	Cherry	Laurel	Irons
Green	Mellon	Elder	Nichol

The names of seasons are quite common, as:
Spring, Sommers, and Winter, and even Mr. *Fall* is encountered occasionally.

Characteristics

Names like the following are heard often. You can impress many such names upon your mind by giving them momentary thought. They convey a definite idea:

Small	Olds	Early	Young
Biggs	Best	Meek	Worst
Bright	Coy	Strong	Lucke
Close	Sly	Savage	Swift

Occupations, Trades, Professions

There are many such names, but I will present only a few. Grasp the significance in names of this kind, when you hear them:

Baker	Carpenter	Mason
Barber	Doctor	Miller
Butcher	Fisher	Sawyer
Cooper	Gardner	Shepherd

Mr. *Weaver's* picture is shown on the next page.

Advertised Names

Many names can be fixed in the mind by linking them with something with which you are well acquainted.

MR. WEAVER

You have in your mind a large group of names which have become known to you through advertisements. You are familiar with the name and the article advertised with it.

Ford suggests immediately a *mind's-eye* picture of an automobile. When you read the name Gillette you picture a safety razor.

So when you meet a man with a name that has become well known to you through advertising, make use of this familiarity.

Picture Mr. Ford with a Ford auto, or Mr. Gillette using a safety razor, or Mr. Kellogg holding a package of cornflakes.

Well-Known Articles

The name of a well-known article frequently flashes into your mind upon hearing a stranger's name. For example, Mr. Waterman may have reminded you of the fountain pen.

As you are now paying more attention to names, similar experiences will occur more frequently. A realization of this familiarity—this association—in itself will go far towards fixing the name in mind.

The accompanying picture is that of Mr. *Eaton.*

You can recall his name when you again meet the picture.

MR. EATON

Other Examples

Armour suggests *meat.*
Remington " *typewriter.*
Heinz " *pickles.*
Wilton " *rugs.*
Snider " *catsup.*
Welch " *grape juice.*

Geographical Names

You meet many people who have the name of some country, state, city, street, or geographical location. For example:

Mr. Ireland suggests *Ireland.*
Mr. Paris " *Paris, France.*
Mr. Patterson " *Paterson, N. J.*
Mr. Richmond " *Richmond, Va.*
Mr Billings " *Billings, Mont.*
Mr. Bleeker " *Bleecker Street.*

At times the spelling is slightly different, but the sounds of the two names are similar.

LESSON THREE 85

If you meet a stranger by the name of Cleveland, you can associate him with the city of the same name. If familiar with Cleveland, Ohio, you can picture the man in some definite part of the city. These geographical *reminders,* however, do not require you to know the exact location. The fact that you associate the stranger with something *definite* is of great help.

Do not form the idea that you will be confused when you recall the name. A little practice with the process described in this lesson will prove of much value, regardless of any experience you may have had in the past with an occasional use of similar methods. Regular application and practice brings results.

Historical and Political Names

You frequently meet strangers with familiar names, such as Lincoln, Grant, Bryan, Wilson, or many others that are well known.

Impress upon your mind the fact that the stranger's name is the same as that of the well known personage.

As you see the face of the stranger, Mr. Grant, for example, your *mind's eye* should form a picture of General Grant. This process will fix the two faces in your mind, and later will help to recall the stranger's name.

But you must be alert and actually form the *mind's eye* picture of the historical or political personage at the time when you see the stranger's face.

MR. LAWRENCE

Here we have Mr. *Lawrence.*

You will meet him later and be asked to recall his name.

Other Names Have a Double Reminder

C l e v e l a n d may suggest Cleveland, Ohio, and former President Cleveland.

J a c k s o n may suggest Jackson, Michigan, and also Stonewall Jackson.

L i n c o l n may suggest Lincoln, Nebraska, and also Abraham Lincoln.

Every added *reminder* or link in your association makes it easier to recall the name.

It is quite possible that these names may convey entirely different thoughts to you. Lincoln may bring to your mind some friend or relative whose given or family name may be Lincoln. Patterson may remind you of the president of the National Cash Register Company, or of some acquaintance by the same name.

The main thing is to make names remind you of something definite and to picture the idea suggested. Then you will have a known image in your mind associated with the face.

Familiar Names

Many names will immediately bring to your mind the faces of friends or acquaintances. You can see them

Lesson Three

clearly in your *mind's eye,* as the names are mentioned. This affords you one of the best means you have for fixing names in mind.

You may meet a stranger named Johnson. The name will remind you of a Johnson you know. The act of thinking and picturing the familiar Johnson, while looking at the stranger, links the two names.

In other words, you will have the two Johnsons associated in your *mind's eye.* The next time you meet the new Mr. Johnson, the original man by that name will probably be recalled and give you the name.

Form the habit of associating the stranger with your friends or acquaintances who bear the same name. You will soon employ this means with scarcely any conscious mental effort.

Transforming Names

There are many names in which a few imaginary changes will produce striking results.

Mr. Boyle	becomes	Mr. Boil
Mr. Barbour	"	Mr. Barber
Mr. Howell	"	Mr. Howl
Mr. Nayler	"	Mr. Nailer
Mr. Cole	"	Mr. Coal
Mr. Holloday	"	Mr. Holiday
Mr. Hyde	"	Mr. Hide
Mr. Stahl	"	Mr. Stall

This is Mr. *Rohr*.

It is far easier to remember a name if we can find a likeness to something we know.

Reminders

MR. ROHR

The mind grasps and retains things we understand. Many names devoid of meaning will suggest familiar words if we make an effort in this direction.

With a slight change in spelling, and the use of imagination, we change the name

<pre>
Bassett   to basket   Buckley to buckle
Cameron   "   camera   Quigley "   quickly
Parshley "   parsley   Sarden "   sardine
Seymour   "   see more   Sieberts " sea birds
Schaefer "   shaver   Skelton "   skeleton
</pre>

When you meet Mr. *Bassett* and note that the name is similar to *basket,* you have something in mind that helps you to recall the name. In other words, *basket* reminds you of *Bassett*. It is what I term a *reminder* for the name. *Camera* is a reminder for *Cameron* and *parsley* reminds me of a man named *Parshley*.

Making Reminders Is a Natural Process

The use of *reminders* is natural with all minds. Many people do not realize that they ever use this simple principle.

Lesson Three

You can find *reminders* for all names. It all depends upon the effort and the imagination you put forth.

This is Mr. *Bauer*.

Merely *reading* the suggestions I have given you, without putting them into practical use, will not be sufficient to overcome a poor memory for names. But these principles, plus proper thought and application, will bring about a wonderful improvement.

Just remember this—always make names suggest definite ideas. Then you will find it possible to remember many names that have bothered you for years.

MR. BAUER

Make Reminders for the Following Names

Farmer	Townsend
Butler	Whitney
Holden	Hughes
Hallford	Seymour

First Syllable Reminders

Some men recall names by the use of the alphabet. In trying to recall a name, they start with *A* and run through the alphabet rapidly until they come to the letter that sounds familiar. Through this letter they are able to recall the name. This method is crude and unreliable, though helpful at times.

While the first letter is of aid, the first syllable is a strong *reminder*.

MR. HOLDEN

Take advantage of this fact and you will find many apparently difficult names that can be fixed in mind readily.

The first syllable frequently has a definite meaning. This can be pictured and associated with the face.

For example, *hay,* the first syllable, will help materially to recall the name *Haydon.*

This is a valuable principle and should be applied whenever possible.

Other First Syllable Reminders

Allison	suggests	Alice	Mendenhall suggests	Mend
Bernida	"	Burn	Noonan "	Noon
Chernook	"	Churn	Pittock "	Pit
Dineen	"	Din	Raney "	Rain
Eaton	"	Eat	Sandvall "	Sand
Funston	"	Fun	Talbot "	Tall
Grimshaw	"	Grim	Whipple "	Whip
Hegberg	"	Egg	Lambert "	Lamb

The above picture is that of Mr. *Holden.* Use the first syllable, *hole,* to assist in fixing the name in mind.

Lesson Three

Memory

Use the Method Best Fitted for Your

Minds differ. Try the various means, and find those best suited for your memory. It is well always to link a name with some one or something you know. This mental effort, though usually very slight, will go far to impress the name.

Reminders for names—as you have already seen—are a valuable help. Practice on names. See what they will suggest. Make *reminders* for them. It is quite easy with many names. Here are a few more illustrations. You can increase your ability to remember names if you will analyze them in a manner similar to these.

Additional Reminders

Alban	suggests	Albany
Bankenship	"	Bank and Ship
Copenhafer	"	Copenhagen
Disston	"	Distant
Eshelman	"	Ashman
Forek	"	Fork
Gleason	"	Glisten
Herzinger	"	Hurt Singer
Laskar	"	Alaska
Mallon	"	Melon
Padgit	"	Patch it
Regnor	"	Reckoner
Sharman	"	Charming
Thurston	"	Thirsty
Sackett	"	Sack it
Wolcott	"	Wall Cot

Difficult Names

Difficult names are usually of foreign extraction. They should prove easier to those who are acquainted with one or more foreign languages. An alert mind and a good imagination will make many foreign names easy to grasp.

Use your imagination and make reminders—through similarity of sound—for names that do not convey any meaning.

Migliavacca sounds like *Milwaukee*, with an added *g* before the *l* of Milwaukee.

Darowitch suggests *Dervishes*.

The simple name *Carey* was easily remembered when the student thought of the sailor's phrase—*Mother Carey's Chickens.*

Capek recalled a familiar trademark—*Apex*.

Quartermas suggested *porterhouse* to one of my students, although *quartermaster* would have been better.

A pupil could not remember the name *McHenry* until he thought of a man named *Henry*, who worked for a man known as *Mac*. This proved a good *reminder* for *McHenry*.

Another difficulty was in remembering the name *Percheron*, the breed of a horse owned by a man named Robbins. The picture of a *robin* perched on the horse—in other words, a *percher-on*—fixed the name in mind.

Another student had trouble with the name of the French General, *Humbert*, until he associated the name with the *hum* of bullets and a friend named *Bert*.

The following article which touches on a few Irish

names may prove of interest and open up a new line of thought for you:

Origin of Irish Names

If your name is Murphy it means that you are "superior," for that is the derivation of the word, just as Kelly came from O'Kelly, Kiely, Keeley, meaning "for war"; O'Connor from Connors, Conerty, meaning "helper"; and Dougherty from O'Doherty, Doherty, Daughaday, meaning "destroyer." Nearly all Irish names at the first stage in their history had "O" before them, the first change consisting of dropping that "O." Sullivan was originally Sillifant and Sullivant, meaning "quick-sighted"; O'Donnell and McDonnell and all combinations of that name were Donald, Daniel, Dona, meaning "dark chief"; Maloney was O'Mullowney, Meloney, Mullany, meaning "thoughtful"; McCormack was O'Cormac, McCormac, McCormick, meaning "sons of the crown"; Flynn was Flann, meaning "red"; Flannigan was Finnegan, meaning "Druid"; Boyle was Boylan, Boland, Bolan, Boylin, meaning "benign"; O'Brien was Bryan, Bryant, Brines, Byron, meaning "author."

This is Mr. *Whitney*.

Fear of Ridicule Spoils a Good Method

Do not be afraid of forming *reminders* because you may happen to know of cases where laughable mistakes occurred by this method. For instance, calling:

Mr. Hornblower, *Blowhard*
Mr. Woodhead, *Blockhead*
Mr. Cassell, *Palace*
Mr. Sturgeon, *Fish*
Mr. Philbert, *Nut*

MR. WHITNEY

Such mistakes have happened. The trouble was not with the method but with the lack of practice. Regular use of the common-sense method of *reminders* will soon overcome any such difficulty. *Every memory needs reminders.*

Business Reminders

A man's business is usually easier to remember than his name.

The business or profession suggests a definite idea, while the name frequently means nothing. Names and occupations sometimes present humorous combinations.

The following are of this nature:

Mr. *Shearer* and Mr. *Shaver* operate a *barber shop*.

Mr. *Drew* and Mr. *McCash* are in the same *bank*.

Mr. *Burns* is a *fireman*.

Mr. *Condit* is an electrician, suggesting *conduit*.

Mr. *Fitz* is a *clothier*.

Mr. *Gallup* owns a *livery stable*.

Mr. *Heady* is a *barber*.

Mr. *Ketchum* is a *truant officer*.

Mr. *Lindsay* is in the oil business, suggesting *linseed oil*.

Mr. *Abel Crook* is an *attorney*.

Mr. *Seitz* is an attorney—*cites* cases.

Mr. *Wildhack* sells automobiles.

While examples of this nature are somewhat uncommon, many similar combinations may occur.

The Business Suggests the Name

The ease with which a man's business is recalled can be made the basis for remembering his name. The following illustrations show how such associations can be of help.

These are all practical applications that have been made by myself or by students.

Mr. *Booth* is the buyer in a large company. His little office, a *booth*, suggested his name.

Mr. *Cooley* represents an electric company. He sells electric fans that make one *cool*.

Mr. *Merrill* is the publisher of a comic paper. Comic papers make us *merry*.

Mr. *Walker* is a reporter. It is natural to think that a *reporter* must be quite a *walker*.

Mr. *McLean* is a city engineer. One of the duties of a city engineer is to *make lanes*.

Mr. *Brown* is a baker—suggesting the thought that he bakes nice *brown* loaves of bread.

Mr. *Cook* was succeeded by Mr. *Camp* in the *Icy Hot Co.* There is a natural association between *cook, camp* and *hot* which was helpful to a student.

Mr. *Furnas* is an ice cream manufacturer. The name was associated with his business by thinking that a *furnace* is no place for ice cream.

I could cite hundreds of similar cases where a momentary thought fixed the name in mind. The foregoing give you the idea. Apply this method when possible.

Circumstances of Meeting

You can sometimes remember names through the circumstances attending the meeting. Were you to meet Mr. *Parsons,* Mr. *Sexton,* or Mr. *Pugh* at church, the place of meeting would serve to fix the name in mind.

Meeting Mr. *Morgan,* Mr. *Rich,* or Mr. *Gould* at a bank might later suggest the name if you noted the association.

At a party where the guests wore Indian costumes, a student met Mr. *Pownell.* The Indian party naturally suggested *Pow Wow.* This served to fix the name indelibly in mind, although the student's memory for names had been wretched.

Rhymes as Aids

Many simple devices can be used to strengthen name impressions.

Some minds are specially impressed by rhymes.

Mr. *Hicks,* in the shoe business, suggested *"Hicks* sells *kicks."*

Mr. *Scruggs,* a druggist, suggested *"Scruggs* sells *Drugs."*

Mr. *Spence,* in the rental business, suggests *"Spence Rents."*

Mr. *Heath* was met at *Keith's* theatre. Later this similarity of sound served to bring back the name.

Descriptive Reminders

Descriptive words beginning with the same letter as the name may be helpful.

Mr. Smith may not suggest anything definite, but *Sober Smith* or *Smiling Smith* may help to describe and identify the individual.

Descriptive *reminders* like the following may suggest other ways in which you can fix names.

    Jovial Johnston   Banker Bloss
    Courteous Culberson Spare Sperry
    Good Gorman   Watchful Watt

Remembering Initials

Initials are harder to keep in mind than names. They express nothing, as a rule, and of themselves form no definite picture. There is, however, a simple way by which they can be fixed in mind.

Initials that occur in alphabetical order, such as A. B. Carson, R. S. Thomas, G. H. Ingalls, are easily remembered.

Words from Initials

Initials and the first letter of the name frequently spell words that make excellent *reminders*. For example:

    B. A. Graham...............*Bag*
    C. O. Branch...............*Cob*
    D. E. Light................*Delight*
    M. U. Duncan..............*Mud*
    S. T. Arndt................*Star*
    Y. E. Sinclair.............*Yes*

You may go even further, and note that *B. A. Graham—Bag—*is quite a talker—a wind-bag.

George O. Wildhack is an automobile dealer in Indianapolis. *GO Wild Hack* will be kept in mind readily.

G. W. Thompson suggests *George Washington* Thompson.

Uncertainty Overcome

One of my instructors had in his class a father and son by the name of Gaffney.

The father was a large man and his initials were C. B.

C suggested See, B suggested Big. He was recalled as *See Big* Gaffney—C. B.

The son's initials were C. L., and, as he was a smaller man, he was designated as *See Little* Gaffney.

An attorney had two brothers as clients. Their names were G. Barton and L. Barton.

Upon meeting either one it was difficult for him to tell whether it was G. or L.

He finally was able to distinguish them by noting that their occupations suggested their initials

G. Barton sold *g*rain.

L. Barton sold *l*umber.

Initial Reminders

Initials may also suggest phrases, as:

E. C..........Easy
L. C..........Elsie
K. C..........Casey
H. N..........How nice
G. B..........Good boy
P. G..........Pretty good

Other combinations of initials may suggest familiar abbreviations, as:

    M. D......Doctor
    P. S.......Post Script
    N. J.......New Jersey
    S. F.......San Francisco
    C. E.......Civil Engineer
    B. A.......Bachelor of Arts
    P. M......Postmaster or Afternoon
    A. M......Ante Meridian or Morning

Names Associated with Appearance

Many people have prominent features or characteristics. This gives the observant student a helpful means for associating the name. The method requires observation and practice only. It can be applied oftener than you may think possible.

If you meet Mr. *Short,* and he is a *short* man, note this fact.

You may meet Mr. *Brown,* and observe that his hair is decidedly *brown.*

Mr. *White* may have *white* hair or moustache, or have blond hair, which can be made the means of recalling the name.

The following are a few of many illustrations that I have noted:

Mr. *Post* is unusually tall, suggesting a large *post.*

Mr. *Biggar* is also above normal height. He is *bigger* than the others.

Mr. *Long* is very tall—a *long* man, and is the subject of many jokes because of his name.

Let me introduce the following gentlemen. Make strong *reminders* and *associations*. You will meet them again.

MR. SEYMOUR

MR. FARMER

MR. TOWNSEND

MR. HUGHES

Contrast Also Effective

The appearance of the person is frequently in direct contrast to the implied meaning of the name. This contrast, if noted, makes a forcible impression upon the mind.

Mr. *Small* is a *tall* man.
Mr. *Stout* is *slender,* not stout.
Mr. *Day* is dark as night.
Mr. *Gay* is decidedly *solemn.*
Mr. *Withers* is *stout,* not withered.

You will find many opportunities for associations such as these, and the ones to follow. Be alert and observant. Use your imagination and your *mind's eye.*

MR. FORKER

Characteristics

The appearance or characteristics of many people may be suggestive of the name.

We have all met a Mr. *Young* who looked *old.* We have also met Mr. *Young* who was *young* looking.
Mr. *Stern* may have looked quite *jolly.*
Mr. *Jolly* may have looked *stern.*
Mr. *Frazier* is cold looking, suggesting *freezer.*
Mr. *Friendly* has a *friendly* appearance.
Mr. *Hart* is big and kind-hearted—*hearty.*

Mr. *Kurtz* is *curt* in speech.
Mr. *Sauers* is a scowling, *sour* looking person.
Mr. *Noyes* is a loud talker—*noisy*.
Another Mr. *Noyes* may be unusually quiet.
Mr. *Begg* is prosperous looking—does not *beg*.

Hanson and *Hansen* are names heard frequently. They sound much like handsome. If you will stop and ask yourself "Is he really handsome?" your hold on the name will be quite secure.

The important thing is to take a second or two and do something *definite* with the name.

This is Mr. *Butler*.

MR. BUTLER

Names Frequently Suggest a Joking Remark

Mr. *Younger* may be greeted with "You surely look it."

Mr. *Cross* will be met with "You seem pleasant enough."

Mr. *Baer* frequently hears "He's a bear."

Associating Name and Personal Appearance

While all people do not lend themselves readily to association, *opportunities for linking names and appearances are abundant.* Take advantage of them.

Lesson Three

Every illustration used is an actual case from life, and there are many more that could be given. Read them all carefully, and form a definite mental picture of each illustration.

Associating Name, Color, Complexion, or Characteristics

The name in many instances is directly suggested by the appearance, such as Mr. *Gray* having noticeably *gray* hair. Mr. *Cole,* or Mr. *Coleman,* may be dark, almost *coal* colored. Mr. *Dyer* has black hair, suggesting *dye.*

Color Illustrations

Mr. *Bailey* is unusually pale, suggesting *p a l e y* .
Mr. *Leitz* is dark—by contrast, *l i g h t* .
Mr. *Redfield* has a sandy beard, suggesting a *r e d f i e l d* of hair.
Mr. *Ruddiman* has pink cheeks, suggesting a *r u d d y m a n* .
Mr. *Schwartz* has a dark complexion—is *s w a r t h y.*

Blemishes, Scars, and Wrinkles

Mr. *Pierce* has a deep scar, suggesting *p i e r c e d* .
Mr. *Nicholson* has a deep dimple, suggesting *n i c k* .
Mr. *Lyons* has many wrinkles, suggesting *l i n e s* .

Beard and Hair

Mr. *Baldridge* is bald, suggesting a *b a l d r i d g e* .
Mr. *Bristol* has a bristly moustache, suggesting *b r i s t l e* .

Mr. *Harrison* is bald—the *h a i r i s g o n e*.

Mr. *Waring* has thin hair—it is *w e a r i n g o f f*.

It is not a good idea to associate the name or face with clothing or dress. When you see the person in different attire, you will miss the former association.

When you use a personal feature or characteristic you are on the safe side.

We can link a name like *Hartley* with the fact that he has *hardly* any hair left. The observant person on next meeting Mr. *Hartley* will recognize the face, which will recall the appearance of his hair, even though it may be covered by the hat.

Forehead and Eyes

Mr. *Bickford* has a prominent forehead, suggesting *b i g f o r e h e a d*.

MR. HALLFORD

This is Mr. *Hallford*.

Mr. *Dolley* has doll-like eyes, suggesting *d o l l y*.

Mr. *Goodnow* has a large forehead, suggesting *g o o d k n o w*.

Mr. *Pearson* has large piercing eyes—*p i e r c e*.

Mr. *Keene* has sharp eyes —*k e e n*.

Use the means you find the easiest. Instead of noting

Mr. *Keene's* bright eyes, you may remember him as appearing keen.

Chin, Nose, and Mouth

Mr. *Fisher* has a hook nose, suggesting *f i s h e r*.
Mr. *Furman* has a firm mouth—*f i r m m a n*.
Mr. *Hill* has a large nose, suggesting *h i l l*.
Mr. *Monteith* has gold teeth—*m o n* (ey) *t e e t h*.
Mr. *Phillips* has full lips, suggesting *f u l l l i p s*.
Mr. *Wilson* has a firm chin, suggesting *w i l l*.

Ear Associations

It is interesting to notice ears. They are excellent means for identification. No two pairs are alike. The confusion of mistaking strangers for acquaintances may be avoided by carefully noting the ears.

Mr. *Hurd* had large ears, suggesting *h e a r d*.
Mr. *Turner's* ears curled over, suggesting *t u r n e a r*.
Mr. *Finn* had large ears, suggesting *f i n s*.
Mr. *Rodenbach's* ears were far back,—*r o d e i n b a c k*.
Mr. *Littler* had large ears, by contrast—*l i t t l e r*.

Let me repeat that these means cannot be used at all times. Looking for something with which the name may be associated is of great help. It improves your power of observation and the ability to make associations.

Double Associations

When you form several associations it will give you a better hold on the name and face.

Mr. *Lacy* may appear *lazy*—or *energetic*, not *lazy*—and his hair, eyelashes or eyebrows may suggest *lacy*.

Mr. *Silver*, a *jeweler*, may have *silvery* hair.

Mr. *Bell's* face may be *bell*-shaped, and his voice as clear as a *bell*.

Mr. *Stumpp* is short and stout, *stumpy*, and his moustache is cropped off close, looks *stumpy*.

Dismiss any idea that you may have formed as to the danger of mistaking names when associated in this way.

Making Names Stick

Some people have a way of making others remember their names. A certain salesman always introduces himself: "My name is *Cable*—not a *rope*."

Another impresses his name, saying "*Cawthorne* is my name—just think of *Hawthorn*."

A former student, years ago, met a man named Barfield, whose name he could not remember. Finally Mr. Barfield said, "I'll fix it so you never can forget it. My name is *Barfield*—think of *Garfield*." From that day to this, he has never forgotten the name.

Mr. *Strickland* says "Think of *strychnine*."

Mr. *Harnecker* impresses his name by telling you to think of *arnica*.

Help people to remember your name, if necessary, by giving them some reminder for it.

Thousands of my students have already improved their memories for names as well as faces by following the suggestions in these lessons. The use of the suggestions will accomplish wonders for you. It requires only momentary thought upon meeting strangers, and the reward in satisfaction—not to say anything about the business value—is great.

Memory for Faces

To remember names you must of necessity remember people. To remember people you must have a good memory for faces.

If your face-memory is poor, you must observe faces carefully. Try to note every feature. Look away from the person for a moment and see if you can form a *mind's-eye* picture of the face.

Then compare this impression with the actual appearance of the face. After you have left the person, occasionally recall your mental image of the face.

Form this habit of observing carefully and *recalling* the appearance of people. Use your faculties as they should be used, and actually *see* faces and features. Your improvement will be marked.

Collect Pictures

It is a good plan to cut illustrations of people from the better grade of magazines, and to use them for practice. Increase the size of your collection as your ability improves. Put the name on the back of the clipping, and make definite associations.

Review these pictures frequently, especially those with which you experienced difficulty. Some of my students have gradually enlarged their collections to five hundred pictures, upon which they practice regularly. In this way they have developed remarkable ability for remembering names and faces.

See the Name

If possible, always try to see in the *mind's eye* just how the name would appear if written or printed.

Writing the Name

Writing the name and looking at it carefully, while recalling the face of the person, is also of value. One of my students always prints the name, for he says the effort involved in printing helps to place the name firmly in mind. Another student writes it with his left hand, and the attention required helps him fix the name.

Repetition as an Aid

I suggest that after having heard the name of a stranger, the name be used as frequently as consistent in the conversation. It helps to fix the name in your own mind and at the same time conveys a favorable impression upon the other person.

Keep a Record

The principle of *recall* is of the greatest importance in remembering names. You rarely have trouble with the names of people whom you meet frequently.

An occasional *mind's eye* recall of people serves the same purpose as actually meeting them. It keeps the names in mind, even though you do not meet these people for years.

Lesson Three

Many students carry a card for writing the names of the people met every day. At the close of the day the *mind's eye* image of every person is recalled.

This is exceptionally good practice, and will work wonders for you in increased ability.

Recalling the name and face is like meeting the person many times. Soon such names and faces will be like old friends.

SUMMARY OF LESSON THREE

1—The visual impression of the face is a strong one. On the other hand, the impression of the name coming through the ear is a light one. By using the various principles outlined you can convert the name-impression into strong visual-impressions.

2—Names are so arbitrary and so widely different that it is necessary for you to strengthen the impression of the name in as many ways as you can.

3—Be sure to take advantage of every method that may help you to impress a name. Add to the means I have given you any others that will be of assistance.

4—Remember that a mental picture will live long after meaningless words have been forgotten.

5—When you hear a name always think whether you have ever heard or read it before. This quickly becomes a helpful habit.

6—Bear these principles well in mind:
    a. Attention.
    b. Observation.
    c. Association.
    d. Make a name mean something.
    e. Last but not least—make the effort.

Recall These Names

These are the sixteen men you met in the course of the lesson. Now call every one of them by name. If you have difficulty with any, form new associations.

Lesson Three   111

LESSON THREE 113

PRACTICE CHART 4

Write names of five acquaintances whose names have a meaning.
_____
_____

Write five names familiar through *Advertising*.
_____
_____

Write five names familiar through *History or Politics*.
_____
_____

Write five names familiar through *Geography*.
_____
_____

Write five names that can be associated with business or appearance of the person.
_____
_____
_____

What reminders can you form for the following names?

GREASON_____
BIDDLE_____
CARTER_____
SPELLMAN_____
RECTOR_____
ALLISON_____
GRENOBLE_____
ATKINS_____
MULDER_____
BAXTER_____

Make additional lists of your own.

LESSON FOUR

How to Remember What You Read

Can you read a long article, or a book, and remember it to your satisfaction? If so, you are an exception. Most people find it difficult. The failure is due often to light and careless reading, but generally to not knowing *how to read*—how to visualize and connect the facts and incidents in orderly fashion.

The trouble can be overcome. It *must* be overcome to make the right progress. Books are valueless except for the temporary interest they afford, if what you have read immediately fades away.

The Friendship of Books

Books are close freinds, mere acquaintances, or entire strangers.

Those of you who are booklovers know what I mean without further explanation.

A book is a good deal more than paper and print sewed together and bound in boards. It comes pretty close to being a personality.

Most readers realize that into a book, that is worth while, the author has poured his heart, and soul, and a part of his very life.

Those who would cultivate the habit of reading will find waiting for them—in the great world of books—a host of wonderful friends who will stand by when all ordinary friends fail.

There are also acquaintances in books and newspapers

that are interesting but not worthy of the close study of the friendly books. And the strangers, of course, are the volumes you do not know at all.

In this lesson, I am going to tell you how you can remember that class of reading that is worth all the time you can afford to give it. I am not going to select any particular books. That may be better left to your own judgment and taste.

Abraham Lincoln had but few books. His wonderful character was greatly strengthened by mastering the few that he had. One good book, well read, will give more pleasure and profit than a hundred skimmed hastily.

Few Books Well Read

A wealthy American who has traveled all over the world in his yacht, tells the following story:

He and his party were fishing off the Florida Keys. They were hailed one day by a middle-aged man in a small boat, who asked them for some tobacco. He was invited on board, and his conversation was so interesting that they prevailed upon him to stay a while.

During his visit, he talked of the great literary figures, quoting Shakespeare freely. He spoke familiarly of Homer, Milton, Dickens, and Scott, and recited passages from their works.

The old fisherman, who lived on a small island nearby, was a frequent caller after that, and his wide knowledge of books became a mystery to the party. Finally several of the fishing party called on the old chap in his little cabin, which consisted of one room, scarcely furnished, without a sign of a book.

Puzzled at this, one of the gentlemen said to the old

man: "Pardon my curiosity, but I am wondering where you keep your library from which you have been quoting so interestingly."

"Library?" chuckled the old fisherman. "Why, I have no library. The only book I own is my old school Reader, but I know it by heart."

The old fisherman had time to read carefully, and to master every word and thought in that precious Reader of his. The result was a thorough knowledge of his subject. Similar reading is becoming a lost art.

There are many examples of great men who have obtained all of their education from a few books well read.

How to Remember What You Read

To remember what you read, confine your reading to what is worth remembering. Rapid and careless reading of newspapers, magazines, and light literature is responsible largely for the common failing of forgetting what we read.

Our forefathers had much better memories than we have. They were obliged to use and to cultivate their memories.

Waste of Time

Much time is wasted in superficial reading. This habit has been developed by our quick reading of the daily papers.

We read newspapers to keep abreast of the times, but they have made us careless in our reading.

This bad effect can be counteracted by *careful reading* when you come to matters of importance. In this manner you can acquire a memory that passes over minor details but grasps worth while subjects.

The Quick Eye—The Delinquent Brain

How often has it been your experience that after having read an entire page you cannot recall a single line? The eye read the page but the mind did not co-operate. As a consequence the message was not imparted to the brain. The mind was on a short vacation—thinking of a golf game, a fishing trip, or some business detail. The mind must be made to stay on the job.

Correct This Bad Habit

The tendency of the mind to wander is due largely to the fact that the eye scans the page too quickly. It is necessary to train both eye and mind to work together. The eye must be held in check. The mind must *picture* the printed message.

In other words, we must read slowly, and visualize.

Read Carefully

To overcome a life-long habit of superficial reading, it is necessary to read slowly, and a little at a time.

Always recall the main points, or thoughts of every sentence or paragraph, before proceeding to the next. If the thoughts are not clear, it is advisable to read them again. Surely, if you cannot remember immediately after reading, you will not be able to do so in a few weeks or months.

Understand What You Read

Understand and recall what you have read before turning the page. Frequent pauses, with a rapid mental review of what has gone before, prevents the fading of the impressions we have endeavored to gain.

Follow the plan of recalling carefully the sense of

LESSON FOUR

paragraphs, pages, and chapters. Do not leave any paragraph until you have the meaning clearly in mind.

In this manner you will experience a rapid and surprising improvement in your ability to remember what you read.

Use the Mind's Eye

Your previous exercises in mental picturing will help greatly in remembering what you read. Many things will now present pictures to the mind, with little effort. These pictures will suggest themselves to you automatically.

An author has certain pictures in mind when he writes. He conveys these pictures to you by the use of words, carefully arranged, either in prose or in poetry.

You must use your mind's eye to see clearly the pictures or ideas that the writer had in mind.

In this manner you will realize, as never before, the beauty and the meaning in many selections.

Reading carefully and using the *mind's eye* gives a new insight and an added interest to subjects that previously were dull and meaningless.

Read This Selection

The following selection is taken from "Nature for Its Own Sake," by Dr. John C. Van Dyke. Read it slowly. Stop frequently, and be sure that you picture the descriptions. See every tree, as described, in your *mind's eye*.

> "The spruce, for instance, is a straight-trunked tree that throws out branches that ride upward like crescents, and bear needles that hang downward like fringes. Its outline, when seen in silhouette against the sky, is pyramidal;

its color is dark green, often blue-green when seen from a distance, and at twilight it is cold-purple. * * *

"The black oak grows a straight trunk with limbs that shoot out almost at right angles; but the white oak and the pine oak are crooked and twisted; their harsh trunks are often broken with boles, and their limbs may take angle lines or prong out like the horns of a deer.

"Very different from such an angular growth as the oak is the stately elm, its long limbs branching and falling so gracefully, the weeping willow that throws its branches up and over like the spray from a fountain, the round, ball-shaped horse chestnut, or the long-armed, white-breasted birch of the mountains."

Are you able now to distinguish the difference in the appearance of every tree? If not, go over the first paragraph again, and stop there until you can describe the spruce tree. Continue in the same way from paragraph to paragraph.

The impression will be strengthened if you will take the time to write, in your own words, a summary of the selection you wish to remember.

Let me again call your attention to the importance of understanding every paragraph thoroughly before you pass on to the next.

Now Read This Selection

The following selection from Paul Leicester Ford's introduction to "Sayings of Poor Richard" affords good exercise of your *mind's eye*. Read deliberately and see every article and scene described. Follow the same plan in your daily reading and wherever possible form mental pictures.

"As one handles the little brown pamphlets, so tattered, smoked, and soiled, which constitute so large a proportion of American colonial literature, it needs but small imagination to carry one back into the low-ceiled kitchen, with its great, broad fireplace, around which the whole family nightly gathered—seated on settles whose high backs but ill shut off the cold drafts that entered at doors, windows, and the chinks in the logs or clapboards—their only light the fitful flame of the great fore- and back-logs, eked out perhaps by a pine knot, or in more pretentious households by a tallow dip suspended in its iron holders by a hook in the mantel, the mothers and daughters knitting, spinning, or skeining, with an eye on the youngsters; the sons making or mending their farming tools, or cleaning their rifles and traps."

Read This for Visualization and Association

The following unique selection affords good practice in visualization and association. Be sure and bring your *mind's eye* into play as you read it slowly and carefully.

THE MAGIC LETTER

Did you ever think what a strange letter *S* is? It is a serpent in disguise. Listen—you can hear it hiss. It gives possession and multiplies indefinitely by its touch. It changes a *tree* into *trees*, and a *house* into *houses*. Sometimes it is very spiteful and will turn a *pet* into a *pest*, a *pear* into a *spear*, a *word* into a *sword*, and *laughter* into *slaughter*, and it will make *hot shot* at any time. The farmer has to watch it closely. It will make *scorn* of his *corn,* and reduce every *peck* to a *speck*. Sometimes he finds it useful. If he needs more room for his stock, it will change a *table* into a *stable* for him, and if he is short of hay, he can set out a row of *tacks*. It will turn them into *stacks*. He must be careful, however, not to let his *nails* lie around loose. The serpent's breath will turn them into *snails*. If he wishes to use an engine about his farm work, he need not buy any coal or have water to run it. Let the serpent glide before his horses. The *team* will turn to *steam*. If you ever get hurt, call the serpent to your aid. Instantly your *pain* will be in *Spain*. Be sure to take it with you the next time you climb a mountain if you desire to witness a marvel. It will make the *peak speak*. But don't let it come around while you are reading now. It will make this *tale stale*.

To Memorize Poetry

Poetry is naturally easier to learn than prose, because we have the assistance of rhythm and rhyme.

To memorize either poetry or prose, the main idea, or the last word in one line or sentence, should be associated with the first word, or leading idea, in the following line.

In addition to visualization, which you have already used, notice all points of similarity or contrast, or anything that will enable you to connect the ideas.

In this manner thoughts will follow in regular order, and after a few careful readings you can repeat the exact words of the writer.

Lesson Four

This manner of memorizing is more certain and beneficial than mechanical repetition. We remember the meaning and note resemblances and differences. This method of exercise improves our mental faculties.

Repetition alone, without the use of these other factors, does not simulate mental activity.

You Can Learn This Quickly

The thoughts in the following poem by Jean Brooks Burt cover a wide range of subjects. At first reading these seem difficult to remember.

This poem may be learned quickly through the use of Visualization and Association. Note as you read, the pictures suggested by this poem:

THE THINGS DIVINE

These are the things I hold divine:
A trusting child's hand laid in mine,
Rich brown earth and wind-tossed trees,
The taste of grapes and the drone of bees,
A rhythmic gallop, long June days,
A rose-hedged lane and lovers' lays,
The welcome smile on neighbors' faces,
Cool, wide hills and open places,
Breeze-blown fields of silver rye,
The wild, sweet note of the plover's cry,
Fresh spring showers and scent of box,
The soft, pale tint of the garden phlox,
Lilacs blooming, a drowsy noon,
A flight of geese and an autumn moon,
Rolling meadows and storm-washed heights,
A fountain murmur on summer nights,
A dappled fawn in the forest hush,
Simple words and the song of a thrush,
Rose-red dawns and a mate to share
With comrade soul my gypsy fare,
A waiting fire when the twilight ends,
A gallant heart and the voice of friends.

Remember that your mind works naturally by Visualization and Association.

Now Apply These Principles and Learn the Poem

To connect the first and the second lines of this poem, note the natural association of thought between the words *divine* and *trusting*. Also form a picture of *a trusting child's hand laid in mine*.

Your thought will pass quickly to the different meanings of the word *mine*. It means *my own*, and also an *excavation* in the earth. This suggests the thought of *rich brown earth* being taken from the *mine*. See the *wind-tossed trees* beyond the heap of *rich brown earth*.

Picture clusters of *grapes* hanging on the *wind-tossed trees*. See yourself tasting them. This gives you the cue to the next line—*the taste of grapes*.

Readily associated and pictured with the *grapes* is the next thought, the *drone of bees*. See the *bees* and hear their buzzing about the *grapes*.

The *drone of bees* has a rhythmic sound which will suggest to you *a rhythmic gallop*, from which your thought proceeds. The time for a *rhythmic gallop* is *long June days*. June days are the time for roses, hence *long June days* will give you the next thought, *a rose hedged lane*. Form the picture.

Lovers cause many a smile among neighbors, hence *lover's lays* will suggest a *welcome smile on neighbors' faces*. We can also get the opposite thought from neighbors' faces, namely, *cool* faces. This gives you a start on the following line.

Lesson Four

Open places will suggest *breeze blown fields*, which will suggest the *plover* flying over the fields. The plover's *cry* was caused, we may assume, by the *fresh spring* showers.

This shows how thoughts can be associated. Every student should follow the foregoing plan, form his own associations, and learn the poem.

Later, go back to "The Magic Letter," on page 123, and memorize it by using the same method. See how easily you will be able to link *houses* and *pet*, *pest* and *pear*, and so on.

Learn This Jingle

The rhyming jingle entitled "Forty Signs of Rain" will be of interest to both adults and children. It is full of descriptions which your *mind's eye* can picture.

FORTY SIGNS OF RAIN

The hollow winds begin to blow,
The clouds look black, the glass is low;
The soot falls down, the spaniels sleep,
And spiders from their cobwebs peep.
Last night the sun went pale to bed,
The moon in halos hid her head;
The boding shepherd heaves a sigh,
For, see, a rainbow spans the sky;
The walls are damp, the ditches smell,
Closed is the pink-eyed pimpernel.
Hark, how the chairs and tables crack.
Old Betty's joints are on the rack;
Loud quack the ducks, the peacocks cry,
The distant hills are looking nigh.

How restless are the snorting swine,
The busy flies disturb the kine;
Low o'er the grass the swallow wings,
The cricket, too, how sharp he sings;
Puss, on the hearth, with velvet paws,

Sits, wiping o'er her whiskered jaws.
Through the clear stream the fishes rise,
And nimbly catch th' incautious flies;
The glow worms, numerous and bright,
Illum'd the dewy dell last night.
At dusk the squalid toad was seen
Hopping and crawling o'er the green;
The whirling wind the dust obeys,
And in the rapid eddy plays.

Practice This Every Morning

I wish you to learn the following poem by applying the methods in this lesson. Say it to yourself every morning. Get the spirit of it. The work is good practice, and the poem has an inspirational message.

IT CAN BE DONE
Edward Guest

Somebody said that it couldn't be done,
But he, with a chuckle, replied,
That maybe it couldn't, but he'd not be one
To say so till he tried.
So he buckled right in, with a bit of a grin
On his face—if he worried he hid it.
He started to sing, as he tackled the thing
That couldn't be done, and he did it.

Somebody scoffed, "Oh, you'll never do that—
At least no one ever has done it."
But he took off his coat, and he took off his hat,
And the first thing we knew he'd begun it.
With a bit of a grin and a lift of his chin,
Without any doubting or quit-it,
He started to sing as he tackled the thing
That couldn't be done, and he did it.

There are thousands to tell you it cannot be done,
There are thousands to prophesy failure.
There are thousands to point out, one by one,
The dangers that wait to assail you.
But just buckle in, with a bit of a grin—

> Take off your coat, and go to it.
> Just start in to sing as you tackle the thing
> That cannot be done, and you'll do it.

Make Your Reading a Motion Picture

Follow the simple suggestions outlined in this lesson You will soon find that what you read with an idea of remembering is truly a mental moving picture. And because you can remember the pictures, you can remember what you read.

Put Your Mind in Training

Be deliberate and thoughtful in your reading. You can thus exercise your mind and break it of the bad habit it has acquired of forgetting what you read. Make your eyes travel more slowly, and speed up your *mind's eye,* as you read.

A Written Review

The great secret of a satisfactory retention of your reading is—write your thoughts.

Form the habit of making a brief abstract of the gist of what you have just read.

Make a concise digest in your own language. Then read the article or chapter again and compare it with your own outline. Every time you will do better.

I know many men whose good memories are due to this habit of expressing in their own words the gist of their reading. Impress this idea upon your children, or upon students with whom you may come into contact.

Ear and Motor Memory

There are a few people who can remember better what they hear than what they see. The proportion of so-called *ear-minded* people is small, and for that reason I have paid little attention to the ear memory in these lessons.

But the ear memory can be of help to all of us, especially in reading and memorizing. Reading aloud is of aid because of the impression which is made on the ear memory. Making gestures is also helpful because it helps our motor memory.

A LESSON IN PUBLIC SPEAKING

In my high school and college days I was backward about reciting, or giving a talk. It was with dread that I looked forward to my turn to speak my piece.

Analyzing my reticence, I found it was due to two causes. *Uncertainty* of remembering the subjects for my talk, and the thought that I was not intended for a speaker.

Memory Overcomes Fear

I have learned from my own experience that any one can develop the ability to speak naturally in public. Nervousness in public speaking is usually due to the fear of being unable to say just what you want to say at the right time.

The factor that goes largely to make up confidence is the ability to remember the thoughts you intend to express.

Nearly all public speakers face the same difficulty I faced. Only a few with unusual memory ability are free from this uncertainty.

Until you have investigated this subject you will never

know how much is omitted by speakers of what they had originally planned to say.

Some speakers, under the inspiration of the moment, have the gift of expression—but these are the exceptions.

Preparing on Short Notice

The great, the successful speakers are always able to prepare on short notice.

A Chicago newspaperman told me this story of a prominent New York speaker, who, it is said, always prepares carefully for any talk.

Owing to a mistake on some one's part, he came to Chicago primed for a certain talk. When nearing the city he received a wire from his frantic secretary telling him of a mistake and informing him of his correct subject.

He found that he had about two hours to prepare this new speech. He hired a cab—one of those old-fashioned horse cabs—and requested that he be driven about in a quiet part of the town.

His actions and gestures in preparing his talk frightened the driver, who thought there was something wrong with the man, and drove him to the police station.

As it happened, the newspaper man was at the station, recognized the speaker, and straightened out the matter after a good laugh.

Banish the Fear of Forgetting

Many men, with a natural ability for speaking, are prevented from talking in public by the fear of forgetting something they wish to say.

This fear may be readily overcome by improving the memory. A successful talk is always based upon the ability to remember.

A talk may be learned in two ways: By learning it word for word, or by getting an outline of the points clearly in mind.

Instructions for memorizing the text verbatim have already been given.

Practical Means for Remembering Points

Practical means by which any speaker can remember the points of his talk will now be considered.

Some speakers use a written outline, and have the points noted on a card. There is no harm in this, and it may prevent nervousness, as the outline can be referred to, if necessary.

However, I have seen so many embarrassing situations, due to dependence on written notes, that I advise *doing without them.*

I have watched speakers, who could not distinguish their notes, or who were unable to find the next point, pawing over their cards or papers, to the amusement of the audience and the discomfiture of the speaker.

Many good talks are spoiled in this way. I urge every one to memorize his points if he has the time—and you will see that my method requires very *little* time.

The effect of any talk without the use of written notes is so much more striking that I advise all my students to practice keeping points in mind by the use of the pigeonholes, or the A B C method, explained in this lesson.

Usually, we have plenty of advance notice, and time in which to prepare a mental outline.

An Easy, Dependable Way

I have evolved an easy, quick, and dependable way by which such outlines may be fixed in mind. This method has solved the only problem that was still vexing men who were known as orators—for their thoughts would now and then escape them in an embarrassing way.

I have been asked frequently to assist students in memorizing a talk just about the time they were to deliver it. The time was too short for them to learn the HAT, HEN, HAM series of mental pigeonholes, as taught in Lesson Two.

Hence the A B C Method, which any one can learn and apply in from five to thirty minutes. This method is so simple that it is grasped easily, and requires almost no preparation.

The A B C Memory Code

Every one knows his A B C's. The alphabet presents a Ready Made Outline. It is necessary merely to take advantage of this outline.

I have used the alphabet and selected words that sound like the letters. These words suggest familiar objects and ideas, which are pictured easily.

A B C Words

A—Hay
B—Bee
C—Sea
D—Deed
E—Ease

F—Effervescent
G—Gee (a term used in driving)
H—Hedge
I—Eye
J—Jay
K—Katydid
L—L (elevated railroad)
M—Em (a measure for type)
N—Inn
O—Owe (a bill)
P—Peas
Q—Queue
R—Hour (clock)
S—Eskimo
T—Tea
U—U-boat
V—Vehicle
W—Double U (double you) stooping
X—X-ray
Y—Y (Y. M. C. A.)
Z—Zebra

These words have been selected with a great deal of care.

You can learn them in ten minutes because the *sound* of every letter of the alphabet *suggests the word* to represent that letter. And every word in turn presents a picture.

How to Learn the A B C Code

You must actually see in your *mind's eye* a load of *Hay*, to represent the letter *A*.

You must see a swarm of *Bees*, to represent the letter *B*.

Lesson Four

See a stormy *Sea*, to represent the letter C.

See a man presenting you with a *Deed*, to represent the letter D.

Picture yourself at *Ease*, in a comfortable position, to get the idea of *Ease*, which will suggest the letter E—E's.

See a huge glass of seltzer full of *Effervescence*, which suggests the letter F (*Eff*).

See a driver turning his horse, pulling the reins, and shouting "*Gee*," which suggests the letter G.

Go through the list and form pictures for the rest of the letters in the same manner.

Your imagination will create pictures just as clear for the other letters as have been outlined for the letters A, B, C, D, E, F, and G.

You will observe I have suggested pictures also for the letters L, M, O, R, U, W, and Y.

The other words are so clear that suggestions are unnecessary.

You may be tempted to use substitutes for some of these words, but I recommend strongly that you adhere to this list.

Simplicity Itself

Nothing can be simpler than the association between B and Bee, C and Sea, E and Ease (E's), G and Gee, I and Eye, J and Jay, L and the L road, M and Em, O and Owe, P and Peas (P's), Q and Queue, T and Tea, U and U-boat, and X and X-ray. The sounds are identical.

The other words are fixed almost as easily. After a few repetitions, A will suggest Hay. D will suggest

Deed, F will suggest Effervescent, and so on. It is one of the easiest things you have ever learned, and it is interesting and valuable.

Learn these words. They have been learned in five minutes.

A B C Pictures Learned Quickly

These words may be used as mental pigeonholes in the same way as the code words are used in Lesson Two. The advantage of the A B C words is that they can be learned quickly.

These pigeonholes retain, for instant reference, any ideas that it would be difficult to remember in any other way.

A Valuable Method

The importance of this method cannot be overestimated. Practice is necessary to become familiar with your A B C words. You must learn also to form and recall your picture associations quickly.

Every A B C picture must instantly pop into your mind. You cannot grope for the word when you need it.

The main thing is to see quickly in your *mind's eye* the *picture* that represents the letter.

Mental picturing requires regular practice. By regular practice I mean just a few minutes every day. Then pictures form themselves seemingly without effort.

Enjoyable Practice

You can find real enjoyment in your practice. Ask some one to name ten or fifteen objects. As every one is named link it with an A B C picture.

The method is similar to that explained in Lesson Two. It places the object, or idea, to be remembered in a definite location.

The A B C pictures afford twenty-six definite locations.

Suppose you wish to remember a book, a flag, a collar, and other items.

Book, the first item, is put in the first location, which is *hay*. Form a picture of a *book* and the load of *hay*.

Flag goes in the second place, by picturing a *flag* and the swarm of *bees*.

Collar is fixed in the third place, by picturing a large *collar* and the stormy *sea*.

The other items can be placed, and recalled in regular order, in the same manner.

The A B C words can be used in the same manner as the code words for remembering talks, stories, and other things.

The method is intended primarily for public speakers who have not had the time to learn the regular code words.

The following example will illustrate clearly the use of the A B C words.

How to Plan Your Talk

Supposing you are to make a talk covering the following points in the order outlined.

        1—Organization.
        2—Co-operation.
        3—Competition.
        4—Management.
        5—Distribution.

The word *organization* may suggest a group of men engaged in some particular occupation. In this case *organization*, being the first subject, must be pictured with the load of *hay*.

Your Picture Associations

1—If you will see this group of men—*organization*—unloading the *hay*, you have your first picture.

To some minds, seeing an *organ* on the load of *hay* would be sufficient to recall *organization*.

2—*Co-operation* is the second subject. This must be seen in your second picture, which is the swarm of *bees*.

See the *bees* on the flowers, gathering honey. This suggests *co-operation*.

3—*Competition* is associated with *sea*, by picturing a swimming race—*competition*—in the stormy *sea*.

4—*Management* can be recalled by picturing yourself receiving a large, showy *deed* to a new home—a gift from the *management* for your services.

5—*Distribution* is your last topic. See some one at *ease*, handing out advertisements—making a *distribution* of samples.

Recall Your Pictures

I also direct your attention to the importance of recalling the picture association of the A B C word and the topic.

Before you trust yourself to make a talk based on your A B C words be sure your pictures will come to you instantly and accurately. Review them a sufficient number of times until you are sure of them.

The A B C words will give you a memory on which you can depend, and be self-confident.

You can talk as long as you wish about your first topic, which you have associated with *hay*. You can use any new ideas that come to you under the inspiration that an audience gives you. You do not have to give thought to the topics that follow. You need have no fear of getting off the track. You know when you are through talking about the first topic that it is necessary to think of *bee*. This will give you your next subject.

The topics considered in the previous example present a more difficult problem than the subjects of most talks. They were chosen to illustrate the way in which difficult words can be treated.

Possibly it is a new experience for you to convert into definite picture form such abstract thoughts as *organization, competition, co-operation, management,* and *distribution.*

This is a principle that can always be used. The sketch on page 146 shows how abstract words can be pictured.

Any idea can be reduced to a picture. Any two objects can always be combined in a picture, or a thought connection formed between two ideas.

Picturing Your Talk

In Harper's Magazine of December, 1914, Mark Twain told of the value of pictures in making things stick.

One of my students said he always followed the habit

of picturing what he wished to talk about. He never makes a talk without first formulating his thoughts into a series of mental pictures. He is looked upon as an able and convincing speaker by his club members.

I could cite many instances illustrating the importance of developing your *mind's eye*. It is one of the fundamentals of oral success in any line. It is absolutely necessary for the public speaker.

If you have neglected the drills in Lessons One and Two, and are desirous of improving your ability to talk in public, close this book right now. Begin again with Lesson One and go through your words, carefully forming the mental pictures according to instructions.

A Good Investment

This practice will make your mind quick and keen.

You are making an investment of your time on which you will reap a satisfactory return. While merely reading these lessons will be of value, a little practice will add greatly to your ability.

Note also—and this is important—the drills you receive in forming picture associations create the habit of remembering things definitely and distinctly.

You will be able soon to dispense with this system of mental links and in many instances remember clearly, accurately, and automatically, because of the exercise your faculties have had.

Picturing Without Effort

Your memory will grasp the thoughts that you must go to the court house, telephone Mr. Anson, and keep the engagement with your attorney, by *picturing* without effort on your part, the court house, Mr. Anson, or his location, and the attorney's office.

You must not form your own estimate of the value of these exercises. Understand clearly that these lessons are not the theoretical product of one mind. They are the result of tried, practical, scientific, common-sense applications.

The Value of Absolute Confidence

One of the first students to use the A B C method was a man who had begun recently to make public talks. He had always been timid and afraid to speak in public. He was memorizing a speech, but, although he had gone over it repeatedly, he was not sure of it.

The A B C method enabled him, without any previous memory training, to learn his speeches—and to appear before his audience with absolute confidence.

He now realizes that we all have the God-given power within us to master any task to which we assign ourselves.

In the past few years I have seen many men, who had believed it impossible for them to talk in public, become excellent speakers.

How to Be a Good Public Speaker

Not every one can become a great orator, but every one who has a voice can develop into an earnest, convincing speaker if he so wills.

Knowledge of the subject is half the battle. Knowledge brings with it self-confidence.

Earnestness, knowledge, and self-confidence go hand in hand. The earnest speaker is always convincing.

See things so clearly yourself, that you can picture them for the audience to see. The practice you have already had in visualization will be of great help to you in making the other fellow see what you are seeing in your *mind's eye*.

Speak Distinctly

Clear articulation is most necessary. This you must practice. Pronounce your words carefully and distinctly. I have found it good practice to sound the letters of the alphabet in regular order, speaking every letter clearly.

Pronounce the sounds slowly. Open your lips wide as you begin, and prolong the sound. Take at least two seconds for every letter.

Form the habit of reading or speaking aloud, and pronounce every word carefully and correctly. Do not say *comen* for *coming*. Practice especially on the ending *-ing*, and other endings that so many of us slur.

Correct enunciation is an important factor in public speaking.

Next comes the proper method of delivery. It is almost as great a fault to be too slow as to be too fast.

Be Deliberate

The beginner usually makes the mistake of being in too much of a hurry. In overcoming this fault do not go to the other extreme and become too deliberate.

My advice is to try your talk on one or more friends of good judgment. They can soon tell you whether you talk too fast or too slowly.

If you form the habit of clearly sounding your words, you will almost automatically arrive at the correct speed.

Use Plain Language

Express yourself in plain language. Use short sentences. Many talks go over the heads of the audience because of long words or involved sentences.

Break yourself of the habit of using long words and long sentences.

Few talks are spoiled by being too short. Thousands of speeches are too long. The beginner usually makes the mistake of speaking at too great length. He is given a subject and allotted a certain amount of time. He has prepared for twenty minutes, but he takes thirty minutes or more.

Programs are too long. My advice to speakers, and particularly to the man unaccustomed to talk, is "Always discount your time." If you are given twenty minutes, prepare yourself to use from twelve to fifteen minutes. If given a half hour, do not use more than twenty minutes

The Value of Condensation

You can make a better talk and a better impression if you condense your matter. Properly prepared, most thirty-minute talks could be delivered in ten minutes. A good ten-minute talk always makes a hit.

Get through with your audience before they tire of you. Leave them wishing to hear more from you. It is certainly far more gratifying to have them feel that they would like to hear more than to have them draw a relieved breath when you have finished.

Inexperienced speakers sometimes ramble on because they cannot find a proper stopping place. You can fortify yourself against any such danger by having a few closing thoughts associated with the A B C or code words.

Let this thought sink in—make your talk short—and they will welcome you back.

Brevity is the soul of wit; this is one of the most important facts a speaker can learn. Some speakers never learn it.

What Congregations Like Best

A conceited young clergyman, more celebrated for the length of his sermons than for their eloquence, once asked a famous wit what he thought of the sermon just preached.

"I liked one passage exceedingly well," said the wit.

"Indeed! Which passage was that?"

"The passage I refer to," was the dry answer, "was that from the pulpit to the vestry room."

Good stories are always helpful. They break the ice at the beginning, and they help to drive the points home.

Stories do not "just happen" with most speakers. Much time is spent in selecting and in preparing the proper stories.

A friend once complimented Mark Twain upon the ease with which he related an appropriate story, and remarked that it was wonderful to be able to tell a story in such a manner.

"Indeed," said Mark, "there was nothing easy about it. I told myself the same story in twenty different ways before I found the way that suited me best."

It Pays to Be a Good Conversationalist

The ability to talk in an interesting way has carried many men and women to social and business success. They may have had only a small part of the knowledge of some of those whom they passed in life's race.

When a man holds you spellbound for half an hour or so by merely talking about ordinary subjects, he consciously or unconsciously uses a method to do it.

In order that your interest may be aroused and held, the clever conversationalist makes his points vivid and clear.

A Trained Memory Helps the Tongue

Many men *think* more interestingly than they *talk* or *write*.

You can cultivate the valuable art of conversing by the same methods you have been studying.

You must make your talk clear and vivid. You must dress old ideas perhaps in new garments of imagination. You must use memory and associated ideas.

When anything of particular interest happens to you, such, for instance, as a visit to a great automobile factory, you must visualize it to remember it and make it real again in the telling. Make it all a connected series of events which you can present in an interesting way.

It is difficult to tell you in detail exactly how to learn to converse fluently. But if you will think carefully of just what a real conversation is, you will see that every lesson in this course can be profitably used to such an end.

Anecdotes, poetry or prose, quotations and valuable

data associated in mind by some code word can all be woven into a well rounded conversation.

Picturing Abstract Words

There is no limit to the use of mental pictures. Any word can be made the basis of a picture by using the imagination.

The accompanying sketch shows that it is possible to convert any abstract words into pictures.

SUMMARY

1. Read Carefully
2. Use Your *Mind's Eye*
3. Importance of Recall
4. Selections for Practice
5. Make Your Reading a Motion Picture
6. Make a Written Review
7. Reading Aloud
8. Public Speaking
9. The A B C Code
10. Value of Confidence
11. Important Suggestions
12. The Art of Conversing

LESSON FIVE

How to Remember Figures

Before explaining the code method for figures, I will call your attention to a number of ideas that may be of help in keeping figures in mind.

It is hardly possible for the *average* person to *see* numbers in his *mind's eye,* or to rely upon the ear-impressions for their recall.

However, some figures may be remembered by observing a relationship between the individual digits.

Methods Applicable Occasionally

For example, consider number **2468**. Note that there is a difference of two between every one of the digits. Two added to the initial figure 2 make it four, two to four make six; two to six make eight—2468. The same applies to numbers 1357 and 3579.

There are similar numbers, such as **8642, 7531,** and **9753.** Here again there is a difference of two between every digit, in a descending scale.

Then we have numbers like **1236** and **1348.** Observe here that the first two digits added together in each case make the third, and that the first three added together make the fourth.

The telephone number **7281** suggested two 9s, since 7 and 2 are 9 as are also 8 and 1.

Numerical Relationship

There is a certain mathematical relationship between the digits of the following numbers. The mental process involved in observing these differences may be of help to some persons.

>**1546**—1 from 5 equals 4, 1 and 5 equal 6.
>**4519**—4 from 5 equals 1, 4 and 5 equal 9.
>**1786**—1 and 7 equal 8, 1 from 7 equals 6

I have met a few individuals who remembered numbers in this manner, but I do not consider any of the foregoing methods of much general value.

Figures like **10, 12,** and **25** are used frequently, and, because of our familiarity with them, they are retained with less effort.

Familiar Combinations

Combinations of **12** impress the memory readily because **12** is a number with which we are especially familiar.

Groups like **1236, 1248, 1296, 3648, 2496** are more easily retained because they combine multiples of **12**. **1296** is **12**, and eight times **12**. **3648** is three times **12**, and four times **12**.

Again, **3256** is composed of 32-56. 32 is four times eight, 56 is seven times eight.

Also note **5472**: 54 is six times nine—72 is eight times nine.

A little ingenuity on your part will suggest many other operations by which your grasp on numbers can be strengthened.

Well-Known Figures

The number **57** is associated with certain food products, and suggests a distinct idea. If we had 58 to remember, we might still use the idea of "57," and add 1.

Take **996.** By noting that it is 4 less than 1000, it will be easy to remember.

Certain numbers present combinations of definite ideas. For example, **2176.**

21 suggests the age at which manhood is attained. **76** suggests the date of the year in which the Declaration of Independence was proclaimed—" '76." So we discover that **2176** combines the two familiar ideas.

Similar figures may suggest names, facts, popular stories, dates, familiar addresses, titles of hymns, and many other things.

Other Definite Means

You may wish to recall the sum of **$14.92.** By remembering that Columbus discovered America in 1492—a familiar date—and that the decimal point separates the first two from the last two figures in the amount, the numerals are lastingly fixed in mind.

The height of the Japanese volcano Fujiyama—**12,365** feet—in associated ideas equals **12,** the number of months in a year, followed by **365,** the number of days in a year.

These methods of analysis and comparison, however, have a limited application, and are adapted for use only by certain types of memory.

Dollars and Cents

Quite a number of people remember figures, and especially phone numbers, by converting them into dollars and cents, as:

> 2365 is remembered as $23.65.
> 1489 "   "   " $14.89.

Use this method if it helps you to fix figures in mind. 14 dollars is a definite, familiar amount so is 89 cents. The combination of these two familiar groups is retained more readily by the memory than the mere meaningless figures 1489.

Some Ingenious Methods

Applications of ingenious association to remember figures can be found readily.

A student wishing to retain the phonograph record 17471, "The Man with the Hoe," impressed it as follows:

The man with the hoe started at the age of 17. He used 4 hoes. He was then 71.

The phone number 4838 suggested:

Four ate (4-8); one went away, then three ate (3-8).

The departments in many stores are numbered, and the numbers are combined frequently to represent larger figures.

For example, a department store official remembered the telephone number 3572 by observing that 35 represented the *book* department, and 72, the *jewelry* department.

LESSON FIVE 153

Common-Sense Methods

Some people think it absurd to remember numbers in such a way. But there is nothing ridiculous in the use of these means. It is just common sense. These numbers suggest distinct objects or pictures in the *mind's eye*. This makes it easy and practical to use combinations of these objects, or departments, as reminders for larger numbers.

A Better Way

The suggestions already outlined may be applied occasionally. But those desiring a reliable—an almost infallible means for remembering numbers should learn the number code.

There is a supreme confidence—a joy that comes with a knowledge of the code. Ten or fifteen minutes of daily application for a few weeks are required to master it. You will then be able to carry in mind figures of all kinds, statistics, phone numbers, addresses, dates, and to accomplish surprising feats.

A Good Start

You have already gone far on the road. The exercises in Lessons One and Two paved the way for you. You will see now how easy it is to convert numbers into pictures and pictures into numbers.

The man who can remember figures without the code is fortunate—but nine out of every ten *need* this method. Only the man with the exceptional memory, or the man who does not care anything about figures, can afford to ignore this process.

Interesting and Instructive

You will find the code very interesting and instructive. Unlike the other lessons, however, it will require more application to be of value to you.

To those interested in remembering figures it will prove a revelation. You will see how easy it is to remember figures by the number code.

To those not interested in figures, I make the suggestion that they do not devote much time to the number code part of this lesson.

But remember that the drills and exercises in this lesson are a valuable stimulus to your mind.

Why Numbers Are Difficult

Numbers, of themselves, do not convey clearly defined pictured impressions to the average brain. There is nothing about them to stimulate the imagination.

To be sure, they are duly recorded both through the eye and the ear, but ordinarily they register themselves merely as numbers, which are difficult to retain.

It becomes necessary, therefore, to devise some means by which they may become photographed on our mental films in such a way that they will mean something as definitely as does a word representing an object.

Pictures Will Recall Numbers

We must find something that will represent numbers, and then proceed to fix these substitutes in our minds by practice. Then, when a number appears before us, we shall be enabled to recall at once the *picture* which that particular number represents.

LESSON FIVE

For centuries attempts have been made to find means to fix numbers in mind. The code method is the perfected result of many minds that have worked on this problem. It is a practical method for you—for every one—who wishes to develop a sure memory for figures.

The Number Code

The number code substitutes letters for numbers.

These letters are then combined into words, which readily suggest mental pictures. Most numbers look alike, but there is little danger of mistaking your pictures.

So the basis of an improved memory for figures is to carry them in mind as pictures.

By reading once or twice, in your usual manner, a series of numbers like the following, you will find it difficult to keep them in mind for any length of time:

1971—9958—3537—6838

Using the number code you will have no trouble recalling these numbers at will, for you will carry them in mind by means of the following pictures:

Compare the above pictures and words with the one hundred code words on page 18.

See that *Tub* is word **19**, *Kite* is word **71**—hence the picture of a *Tub* and a *Kite* represents the combination **19-71**.

Simplicity itself—when you know the one hundred words and their corresponding numbers.

The Basis of the Code

The code is based on the **phonetic** or **sound** spelling instead of the actual spelling of words.

Every word is composed of vowels and consonants. The vowels are *a, e, i, o, u,* and have *no figure values*.

In addition to the vowels—which have no figure values—there are three consonants that do not represent figures, namely *h, w,* and *y*. Note that they form the word *why*—which is easily remembered.

These letters—*a, e, i, o, u, w, h,* and *y—are not used to represent figures*.

They are used merely to help in forming words. We can combine them at any time and in any manner desired with other letters without altering the figure value of the word, with one exception.

H, by itself, has no figure value. It, however, helps to form the following combinations: *Ch, gh, ph,* and *sh*. The figure value of these combinations will be explained later.

Consonants Representing Figures

T	represents	1
N	"	2
M	"	3
R	"	4
L	"	5
J	"	6
K	"	7
F	"	8
P	"	9
S	"	0

These letters can be combined with vowels to represent any number. They have been selected because they are similar to the figure they represent or can be readily associated with it.

1—The figure **1** is represented by the letter *T*.
   Suggestion—*t* has 1 down stroke.
2—The figure **2** is represented by the letter *N*.
   Suggestion—*n* has 2 down strokes.
3—The figure **3** is represented by the letter *M*.
   Suggestion—*m* has 3 down strokes.
4—The figure **4** is represented by the letter *R*.
   Suggestion—*r* is the fourth letter in fou*r*.
5—The figure **5** is represented by the letter *L*.
   Suggestion—£, a pound sterling, is about **5** dollars; *L* also represents **50** in Roman numerals.

6𝌆 7K 8β 9P S0

6—The figure 6 is represented by the letter *J*.
  Suggestion—*j* reversed is a roughly formed 6.
7—The figure 7 is represented by the letter *K*.
  Suggestion—note the two 7's forming *K* in the illustration above. One of the 7's is upside down. *K* also follows *J* in the alphabet.
8—The figure 8 is represented by the letter *F*.
  Suggestion—*f* and 8 both have *two loops*.
9—The figure 9 is represented by the letter *P*.
  Suggestion—reverse the loop on *p* and we have 9.
0—The figure 0 is represented by the letter *S*.
  Suggestion—cipher means 0—think of it as sipher. In this way we associate 0 with the *S*—of sipher. Also note that the two parts of *S* reunited as in the drawing form 0.

The illustration shown above will impress upon your *mind's eye* a similarity between certain letters and the numbers represented by them.

Draw all the letters, beginning with *t*, following my suggestions.

Use these, or any other means, to fix the letters and the numerals to which they correspond firmly in mind.

Remember clearly—the following letters have *no numerical value:*

A E I O U—W H Y

LESSON FIVE 159

Now review the code, and see if you have well in mind the numerical value of the letters.

1 2 3 4 5 6 7 8 9 0
T N M R L J K F P S

Having gone this far, I wish to assure you that the code is not complicated. The code words *Hat to Daisies* carry the key. They are formed in accordance with the principles you are now learning. Follow me carefully, step by step.

Additional Letters

You will now learn the figure value of other consonants having a similar sound to those previously considered. Note well:

All consonants having a similar sound have the same numerical value.

1—*T* and *D* have nearly the same sound, therefore both *T* and *D* represent **1**.

6—*G* as in George (known as *soft g*) has the *J* sound, therefore *soft G* also represents **6**. *Sh* as in shot and *ch* as in chain are similar to *j* in sound, so *sh* and *ch* also represent **6**. Note that *h* by itself has no value, but the combination *sh* or *ch* represents **6**. *J*, soft *g*, *sh*, and *ch* all stand for **6**.

7—*C* as in can (*hard* c) is a *K* in sound, therefore *hard c* also represents **7**. *Hard G* as in gay is similar in sound to *K*, so *hard G* also stands for **7**. *K, hard c* and *hard g* all represent **7**.

8—*F* and *V*, when used in any word, sound alike, so both *f* and *v* stand for **8**.

9—*P* and *B* having nearly the same sound, both are used for **9**.

0—*C* as in ice (*soft* c) and *Z* are sounded as *S*. *S, Z,* and *soft C* represent **0**.

Complete Number Code

1—*T* and *D*
2—*N*
3—*M*
4—*R*
5—*L*
6—*J, Soft G, Sh, Ch*
7—*K, Hard G, Hard C*
8—*F* and *V*
9—*P* and *B*
0—*S, Z, Soft C*

It is necessary to be familiar with the sounds of the letters, for as you have already seen, the sound determines the figure value.

C is either *K* or *s*, viz: Cat (*kat*), city (*sity*).
C in cat (*k*) is *hard* c. Its figure value is **7**.
C in city (*sity*) is *soft* c. Its figure value is **0**.
G has two sounds—as in age (*aje*), figure value **6**, and as in *gay*, figure value **7**.
G in age (*aje*) is called *soft g*. Its sound is similar to *ch* in the word much, or *sh* in mash.
J, soft g, ch, and *sh* all have the figure value **6**.

Lesson Five

Words Containing Soft G

Age (aje) 6, hinge (hinj) 26, rage (raje) 46, rouge (ruj) 46, lodge (loj) 56, judge (juj) 66, cage (kaj) 76, page (paj) 96, George (jorj) 646.

Observe *silent* D in lodge (loj) 56, and judge (juj) 66.

It will be good practice to turn to a dictionary and write five or ten other words containing *soft* g.

Note that the *soft* g sound is simply *j*. *J* represents **6**, therefore *soft* g (j) is always **6**.

Hard G

Hard g is similar in sound to *k*, viz: card (*kard*), guard (*gard*).

Pronounce *card, guard,* and you will note that the sounds of *k* and *hard* g are almost identical. Since *k* and *hard* c are **7**, *hard* g, which is sounded almost the same, also has the figure value **7**.

Words Containing Hard G

Gay (7), *egg* (7), *dog* (17), *nag* (27), *fig* (87), *bag* (97), *guard* (741).

Write five or ten other words containing *hard* g.

Words Containing Soft Ch

Ch also has two sounds. *Soft,* in chew (6), *hard,* in ache (*ake*) **7**.

Much (36), *match* (36), *roach* (46), *chain* (62), *chair* (64), *check* (67) *chief* (68), all contain *soft Ch.*

Write five or ten other words containing *soft* ch.

There are few words containing *ch* sounded as *K*. *Ch* nearly always has the figure value of **6.**

Summary

C (s)   *Soft*   C—0.
C (k)   *Hard* C—7.
Ch   *Soft*   —6.
Ch (k) *Hard*   —7.
G (j)   *Soft*   —6.
G (gay) *Hard*   —7.

Letters and Sounds Used Occasionally

The following letters and sounds are mentioned merely for completeness. Make no special effort to learn them now:

Q is a combination of *k* and *w*, viz: Quire (*kwire*), *Q* is **7.**

X (pronounced *eks*) is a combination of *K* and *S*, and therefore stands for **70.** *Ing,* as in king, can be conveniently used for **7.**

By using *ing* to represent **7** you can form more easily words for numbers like 457—railing, 987—paving, 687—shaving, 697—shipping.

Hard ch, as in ache (*ake*) and chasm (*kasm*), has the *k* sound and represents **7,** but is seldom used.

Gh and *ph,* as in rough (*ruf*) 48, and phone (*fone*) 82 have the sound of *f* and represent **8.**

LESSON FIVE 163

Silent Letters Have No Figure Value

In addition to *a, e, i, o, u, w, h, y*, which have no numerical value, *silent letters*—letters that are not sounded in a word—*lose their figure value* in that word.

Therefore, *light* (lite) is **51**—*g* is silent.
Knife (nife) is **28**, *knob* (nob) is **29**—*k is silent*.
Match (mach) is **36**—*t* is not sounded

Pronounce *match* and *much*. You will observe that the *ch* sound is identical, showing that the *t* in match is silent.

Judge (juj) is **66**—*d* is not sounded.
Check (chek) is **67**—*ck* always represents 7.

Double Letters Count as One

Bear in mind: *The number code is based on sound, not on spelling. It is phonetic in all cases.*

We use double letters to represent a single numeral, as if the word were spelled with a single letter, for there is only the single sound.

Note these illustrations carefully:

Hammer (*hamer*) figure value 34
Butter (*buter*) figure value 914
Hill (*hil*) figure value 5
Mamma (*mama*) figure value 33
Boss (*bos*) figure value 90
Arrow (*aro*) figure value 4

How to Use the Code

Having attentively followed the lesson to this point, it will not require much additional effort on your part to learn the words representing every number from 1 to 100.

You have, in fact, been taught these words in Lessons One and Two. You will now see why they have been selected to designate the numbers.

Let us begin with number **1**. This is represented by the letters *t* and *d,* from which we select *t.*

To form a word easily visualized, we can select any of the vowels, *a, e, i, o, u,* and the letters *w, h,* and *y,* and add them to *t.*

Forming the Code Words

For our purpose we have taken the letter *h* and the vowel *a* and combined these with the letter *t* (1). Combining *h* and *a* with *t* into the word *hat* does not change the figure value of *t* (1), for *h* and *a* have no figure value.

In this manner we form the word *hat,* which represents the figure value **1**.

To change *hat* back to the number it represents we recall that *h* and *a* have no figure value, which leaves *t* representing **1**.

Numerous other words could be used for **1**, as *tie, hood, hut, head, dough, toe, wet.*

2. *Hen*—*n* is our code letter for **2**. We have simply added *h* and *e* to make *hen,* whose figure value is **2**.

Lesson Five

3. *Ham*—*m* is our code letter for **3**. We have added *h* and *a*, which have no figure value, forming the word *ham*, which has a figure value of **3**.

4. *Hare*—*r* is our code letter for **4**. We have added *h*, *a*, and *e*, forming the word *hare*, which has a figure value of **4**.

5. *Hill*—*l* is our code letter for **5**. We have added *h* and *i*, and the additional *l*, which is not sounded, forming the word *hill*, whose figure value is **5**.

6. *Shoe*—*sh* in our code is **6**. We have added *o* and *e*, forming the word *shoe*, whose figure value is **6**.

7. *Cow*—*c*, sounded *k*, in our code is **7**. We have added *o* and *w*, forming the word *cow*, whose figure value is **7**.

8. *Hive*—*v* is one of our code letters for **8**. We have added *h*, *i*, and *e*, forming the word *hive*, whose figure value is **8**.

9. *Ape*—*p* is one of our code letters for **9**. We have added *a* and *e*, forming the word *ape*, whose figure value is **9**.

10. *Woods*—*d* is **1**, *s* is **0**. To these we have added the letters *w*, *o*, *o*, forming the word *woods*, whose figure value is **10**.

Cross Out the Letters

Now list these first ten words, and cross out the letters that have no figure value. Then write the number that the remaining consonants represent.

Practice Chart Six will be helpful at this point. It has a complete list of code words that can be used for practice. Cross out the silent letters and vowels. Convert the remaining letters into their corresponding numbers.

Note that the word *snare* is really **024**, but it is used to represent **24**.

Code Words and the Numbers They Represent

1—Hat	26—Hinge	51—Light	76—Cage
2—Hen	27—Ink	52—Lion	77—Cake
3—Ham	28—Knife	53—Lime	78—Cuff
4—Hare	29—Knob	54—Lawyer	79—Cab
5—Hill	30—Moose	55—Lily	80—Vase
6—Shoe	31—Mud	56—Lodge	81—Foot
7—Cow	32—Moon	57—Lake	82—Fan
8—Hive	33—Mummy	58—Loaf	83—Foam
9—Ape	34—Hammer	59—Lap	84—Fire
10—Woods	35—Mule	60—Cheese	85—File
11—Tide	36—Match	61—Sheet	86—Fish
12—Tin	37—Hammock	62—Chain	87—Fig
13—Team	38—Muff	63—Jam	88—Fife
14—Tire	39—Mop	64—Chair	89—Fob
15—Hotel	40—Rose	65—Jail	90—Bus
16—Dish	41—Rat	66—Judge	91—Boat
17—Dog	42—Rain	67—Check	92—Piano
18—Dove	43—Ram	68—Chief	93—Bomb
19—Tub	44—Warrior	69—Ship	94—Bear
20—Nose	45—Rail	70—Goose	95—Bell
21—Window	46—Roach	71—Kite	96—Bush
22—Nun	47—Rake	72—Can	97—Bag
23—Gnome	48—Roof	73—Comb	98—Beef
24—Snare	49—Rope	74—Car	99—Pipe
25—Nail	50—Lace	75—Coal	100—Daisies

LESSON FIVE 167

Code Words and Their Numbers

These words have been selected carefully to represent the numbers between 1 and 100.

Useless Without Practice

You must be able to transpose your code words into numbers without hesitation, and to recall quickly the code word representing any number from 1 to 100. If this is not done any attempt to become familiar with the number code is futile.

Learn the Code Words

You will learn some of the code words more easily than others. Practice on those that trouble you, and you will soon know the figure value of the one hundred words.

If you wish the code word for 82, you know it must contain either *f* or *v* for 8, and *n* for 2. Inserting vowels, try the combinations *vane, vine, fin, fine, fun, fan,* etc. Probably *fan* will be the first word to suggest itself.

To recall the code word for 25, you know it must contain *n* and *l*. The code word for 25 is *nail*.

Any word representing 41 must contain *r* for 4, and either *t* or *d* for 1. The code word for 41 is *rat*.

Review in Groups of Ten

The best way to practice with the code words is in groups of ten. Become thoroughly familiar with the figure value of ten consecutive words at a time. For example, practice with the words *hat* to *woods*, converting them into their respective numbers.

Then transpose the numbers 1 to 10 into the code words. When you know the first ten, practice on every one of the following groups of ten in the same manner.

Then practice with words having the same final number in the following manner:

1—*Hat*	51—*Light*
11—*Tide*	61—*Sheet*
21—*Window*	71—*Kite*
31—*Mud*	81—*Foot*
41—*Rat*	91—*Boat*

Proceed in the same way with the remaining code words, thus:

2—12—22—32, etc.
3—13—23—33, etc.
4—14—24—34, etc.
5—15—25—35, etc.

You Can Transpose Larger Numbers

You can remember larger numbers by combining the code words. To illustrate:

3964 is 39 and 64, represented by *mop* and *chair*.
3251 " 32 " 51, " " *moon* " *light*.
9067 " 90 " 67, " " *bus* " *check*.
1239 " 12 " 39, " " *tin* " *mop*.
795 " 7 " 95, " " *cow* " *bell*.
994 " 9 " 94, " " *ape* " *bear*.

It is necessary only to form a clear picture of *mop* and *chair* to represent 3964.

Lesson Five

The danger of transposing figures, by recalling the picture as *chair* and *mop* 64-39, instead of 3964, can be avoided by having the first object larger than the second. In the case of 3964, picture the *mop* larger than the *chair*.

Another way to avoid transposition of figures is to see the object representing the first figures above the object representing the second figures. For instance, see the *mop* on the *chair*. If the number were 6439 the *chair* would be pictured on the *mop*.

Interesting Practice

Auto and *car numbers, store, office,* and *phone* numbers are excellent material for practice. At first, form words for only the first two figures of automobile numbers. Then take three figures and later form a single word or combination of words for the entire number. Practice at first, on forming words, without trying to remember any, except those that are of especial interest or value.

A Few Additional Words Will Help You

The use of the following words in combination with your code words will make it easier to convert many of the numbers between 100 and 1100 into words. Use one of these words for the first digit and the code word for the last two figures.

1—Hot	Wet	White
2—New	Win	Own
3—My	Aim	Hem
4—Hairy	Wire	Hire

5—Yellow	Oily	Wheel
6—Ashy	Huge	Wash
7—Gay	Weak	Hack
8—Heavy	Few	Wave
9—Happy	Buy	Wipe
10—Dizzy	Hideous	Dose

Become thoroughly familiar with at least one of these words, for every number from 1 to 10, and use it regularly when the combination will permit. You can combine these with your code words to represent numbers between 100 and 1100.

Familiarity with this list and with the code words gives you a firm grip on most figures.

Some Illustrations

138—White muff	618—Wash dove
165—Hot jail	666—Huge judge
263—New jam	738—Gay muff
292—Win piano	799—Weak pipe
343—Aim ram	829—Heavy knob
374—My car	839—Wave mop
441—Hairy rat	935—Wipe mule
476—Wire cage	973—Buy comb
544—Yellow warrior	1018—Dizzy dove
562—Oily chain	1079—Hideous cab

Now see how interesting the subject of figures can be made by picturing every one of the above combinations.

Word Combinations

It is easy to picture the following:

A moon beam.	A shiny bell.
A red chair.	A gray check.
A lean mule.	A bad dog.

It would be rather difficult and uncertain to remember the numbers that these phrases represent, but combinations such as these are readily retained and recalled by mental pictures.

Here are the numbers they represent:

Moon-beam	32-93	Shiny-bell	62-95
Red-chair	41-64	Gray-check	74-67
Lean-mule	52-35	Bad-dog	91-17

When you form such appropriate combinations you have a firm hold on the numbers, through these easily remembered word-pictures.

A Helpful List

The following words will combine readily with most of the code words. There are other words that may suit you better for some of these numbers.

11—Dead	16—Dutch	21—Neat
12—Thin	17—Thick	22—Union
13—Dim	18—Tough	23—Enemy
14—Dear	19—Deep	24—Narrow
15—Tall	20—Nice	25—Only

26—Enjoy	51—Old	76—Hoggish
27—Inky	52—Lean	77—Cook
28—Enough	53—Lame	78—Give
29—Nobby	54—Lower	79—Gabby
30—Messy	55—Loyal	80—Fuzzy
31—Muddy	56—Lash	81—Fat
32—Mean	57—Leaky	82—Funny
33—Maim	58—Leafy	83—Foamy
34—More	59—Leap	84—Fiery
35—Mail	60—Choice	85—Full
36—Mash	61—Jet	86—Fishy
37—Meek	62—Shiny	87—Foggy
38—Move	63—Chummy	88—Heave off
39—Mob	64—Cheery	89—Foppy
40—Rosy	65—Chilly	90—Busy
41—Red	66—Jewish	91—Beady
42—Rainy	67—Shaky	92—Bony
43—Warm	68—Shave	93—Bum
44—Rare	69—Cheap	94—Bare
45—Royal	70—Cozy	95—Blue
46—Rich	71—Gaudy	96—Bushy
47—Rocky	72—Keen	97—Big
48—Rough	73—Calm	98—Beefy
49—Ruby	74—Gray	99—Baby
50—Lacy	75—Cool	

This list will prove helpful for reference. It is not necessary to learn it, but you will gradually acquire many of these words, and add others of your own.

Code Words Used as Verbs

The words *nail, hinge, knife, mail, match, mop,* and many of the code words can be used as verbs. For example:

Nail	a boat	2591	**Mop**	a roof	3948
Hinge	a fan	2682	**Ram**	a car	4374
Knife	a warrior	2844	**Cuff**	a judge	7866
Mail	a pear	3594	**Fan**	a lawyer	8254
Match	a tire	3614	**Bomb**	a jail	9365

You can form a picture of every one of these composite ideas. Do it now.

Mail a *pear* may require explanation, although it is simple. See yourself sticking a postage stamp upon a pear, and dropping it into the post office.

In a similar manner *mail* can be combined with many of the hundred code words to designate numbers beginning with **35**, as:

Mail a **dish** 3516   **Mail** a **muff** 3538
Mail a **knife** 3528   **Mail** a **cheese** 3560

One New Word Instead of Two Code Words

By this time it is doubtless clear that you have the choice of *two* methods in transposing larger numbers:

1. You can use *two* code words, or
2. You can form *one* word to represent the number.

The usual and most satisfactory course in the beginning is to combine your code words. Later you will graduate into the single-word class, almost automatically. Practice will soon make you proficient.

9471

The beginner will represent **9471** by the code words *bear* (94) and *kite* (71). Later he will recognize for 9-4-7-1 the sounds *p-r-k-t*, or *p-r-k-d*, or *b-r-k-t*, or different combinations of these sounds.

The word *bracket* may suggest itself—the *ck* sounded *k* has the value of **7**, not **77**.

If **9471** were a phone number, and you once clearly associated a *bracket* with the person or place, you would have no difficulty in recalling the number.

841

Take the number **841**. Combining the code words for the numbers **8** and **41** would give us *hive-rat*.

It will help you in trying to form a single word for **841** to write the corresponding letter below each number.

8	4	1
f or v	r	t or d

Inserting the vowel *o* we have the word *fort* to represent **841**.

Ford, Friday, freight, fruit, and *avert* also stand for **841**.

321

Try number **321**. Our code word for **3** is *ham,* for **21** is *window*.

To make one word we proceed:

3	2	1
m	n	t or d

Inserting the vowel *i* we have the word *mint*.

Mount, Monday, month, minute, and *mind* are some of the other words that designate **321**.

794

Consider the number **794**. The combination of code words for this is *cow* (**7**) and *bear* (**94**).

794 can also be represented by the single word *copper*.

Among other words for **794** are *cooper, caper,* and *cobra*.

Additional Help in Word-Forming

Note that some words begin with vowels, as *animal* or *enamel* for **235**, *umpire* for **394**, *inlet* for **251**.

If, at first, you cannot form words easily for all numbers, do not be discouraged. Practice will give you most words automatically.

You will soon recognize numbers like **685** as *shovel*, **179** as *teacup*, **648** as *sheriff*, **539** as *lamp*, **939** as *pump*, and so on. This ability will come to you suddenly—like a flash if you will practice.

A Few Minutes Every Day

A few minutes' regular practice every day will be more effective than a long period once in a while. Practice at least a few minutes daily, converting figures into words, and words into figures.

This number study is exceedingly interesting, and is the best kind of stimulus.

Large Numbers

In forming words for the larger numbers you may find it convenient to divide some numbers as follows:

1941—1-941	represented by	**white bird**
2942—2-942	"	"	**new barn**
4016—4-016	"	"	**hire stage**
6142—6-142	"	"	**huge train**
7835—7-835	"	"	**gay family**
8362—8-362	"	"	**heavy machine**

This gives you the choice of representing 1941 by *white bird,* as above, or of combining your code words for 19-41, which are *tub—rat.*

1941 can be designated also by *hot bread, white beard, wet board,* and many other combinations.

Taboret, depart and *tapered* also stand for 1941.

2942 can be represented, in addition to the code word combination, *knob—rain,* as:

no brain,   new born,   own apron.

It will give you valuable and interesting practice to form as many combinations as possible for the above numbers.

You will understand that the object of this exercise is to give you familiarity with the use of your code. In actual use you need form only one combination for any number.

Additional Illustrations

11-30—Dead moose   47-701—Rocky coast
13-47—Team work   94-914—Poor butter
15-96—Tall bush   139-054—Damp cellar

LESSON FIVE 177

18-35—Deaf mule
22-67—Union Jack
35-77—Mule kick
40-18—Horse thief
43-69—Army ship
50-43—Lazy ram
69-74—Cheap car
71-75—Good coal
81-70—Fat goose
84-51—Free light
95-38—Blue muff
97-48—Big roof

143-526—Trim launch
147-014—Drug store
434-951—Armor plate
801-362—Fast machine
846-357—Fresh milk
921-262—Paint engine
948-995—Brave people
950-431—Please remit
957-734—Black camera
20-43-42—Nice warm rain
69-41-82—Cheap red fan
94-75-14—Pure cool water

Consider these words carefully. Understand why they represent the numbers. Go over them several times. Change them into words without referring to the list. You will find additional numbers on *Practice Chart Seven*.

Difficult Numbers

There are some numbers between 100 and 1000 that cannot be represented by a single word. For other numbers it may be difficult, especially for the beginner, to form a word.

If you wish a number for **126** and cannot think of one word quickly, combine the code words for **1** and **26**—*Hat* and *Hinge*.

Visualize a large *Hat* hanging on a *Hinge*, which represents **126**.

Single words for **126** are:

Danish, tinge, tonnage, dingy.

242 can be separated into **2** and **42**. You can combine your code words *Hen* (2) and *Rain* (42), picturing a *Hen* in the *Rain*, for **242**.

Other combinations may suggest themselves for **2-42**, such as

    New horn   **No rain**
    New yarn   **Hen ran**
    Own iron   **Win heroine**

A single word for **242** is:

Neuron

Always bear in mind that the code is based on sound. Note the following:

    262—*nation* (nashun).
    862—*vision* (vishun).

Tion and *sion* are sounded *shun*, hence 62.

You Can Remember Phone Numbers

To illustrate the practical value of our code, we will apply it to telephone numbers. There are probably no figures you are more frequently called upon to remember than these. When you need them you need them at once.

Remembering phone numbers need not trouble you, for the code lends itself remarkably well to the mental filing of such numbers.

We translate the numbers into words and associate them with the name, office, residence or place of business of the person with whom we desire to communicate.

LESSON FIVE   179

A Practical Application

In a Western city are four large stores, with the following phone numbers:

Meier—4600
Woodard—4700
Olds—4800
Lipman—5000

Such numbers are easy to carry in mind when we call them frequently, but I had only occasional use for them.

The final two ciphers presented no difficulty, as I knew these numbers all ended in **00**. I needed only to recall the first two figures.

I fixed them indelibly as follows:

Meier—   **46**—*rush*.   Always a *rush* there.
Woodard—**47**—*work*.   They all *work* here.
Olds—   **48**—*Harvey*. A clerk is named *Harvey*.
Lipman— **50**—*lace*.   The *lace* department is large.

1—The *Meier* store, being the largest, brought to mind the associated thought of *rush*.

R is **4** and *sh* **6**, so rush represents **46**.

This recalls the phone number, **4600**.

2—The *Woodard* store suggested the place where they all *work*.

Since *r* is **4** and *k* **7**, *work* represents **47**, affording a speedy and certain recall of the phone number, **4700**.

3—The *Olds* store brought to mind the name of one of the clerks, Mr. *Harvey*, representing **48**. Adding **00** gives the telephone number, **4800**.

4—The *Lipman* store, having been associated with the *lace* department suggested **50**, the cue for the number **5000**.

Further Applications

A few applications of the number code as used by students in remembering telephone numbers will be helpful.

A railroad—phone number **1784**.

1, 7, 8, 4 can be represented by the letters *t, k, f, r*. From these are formed the words *take far*.

The mind readily grasps the association between a *railroad* and the thought that it will *take* you *far*. Thereafter the particular railroad will instantly reflect the thought *take* you *far*, or *take far*, which, converted into figures, is **1784**.

Appropriate Associations

It is better to form appropriate phrases when possible, but until you have had some practice with the number code you may have to depend, in many instances, upon combinations of your code words, such as *dog fire* for 1784 instead of *take far*.

A bank—phone number, **7191**.

A class member converted the figures **7, 1, 9, 1** into the words *get paid*. I am sure you realize the ease with which this association between *bank* and *get paid* is kept in mind. It is appropriate and readily recalled.

A newspaper—phone number **5510**.

A student suggested the phrase *lie lots* to represent the phone number **5510**. *Lie* is 5, *lots* is 510. Possibly this

Lesson Five

particular newspaper was represented correctly by the thought *lie lots*. You can see that such a phrase, when once associated with the paper, would be recalled readily.

A hotel—telephone, **2068**.

I telephoned to a certain hotel several times, and every time was obliged to refer to the phone book, as I had formed no words for the number, which was **2068**.

I then converted this into the words *nice chef* and formed a mental picture of the *hotel* and a *nice chef*. I shall never forget this association, *nice,* **20**, *chef,* **68**.

A friend, telephone, **4802**.

I fixed the phone number **4802** in mind by the words *rough son*. This description was an apt one, as the family had a boy who was indeed a *rough son*.

I have used phone numbers to explain the process, because of their universal use.

Understand that the same means are at your command to fix any kind of figures in mind with certainty.

Additional Examples in Lesson Seven

Lesson Seven contains additional examples of the application of the code in remembering phone numbers. The exchange is usually not troublesome, but that lesson will show how the exchange can be added to the mind pictures and recalled.

Number Code Application Unlimited

Your watch will not keep time unless you wind it. Neither will the number code serve you until you apply it.

I could give you thousands of illustrations of the use of the number code, but the important thing is to furnish you with the method. It is for you to put it into actual practice on those numbers you wish to keep in mind.

The Code Makes Knowledge Certain

You cannot confuse 98 and 99, because 98 is *beef*, and 99 is *pipe*. They present two entirely distinct pictures, yet 98 and 99 merely considered as numbers are readily confused.

As an illustration of this I cite a recent experience. I have occasional use for the address **12—99th Street.**

Uncertainty Overcome

When I tried to recall the street I was uncertain whether it was 98th or 99th. Then my mental picture came to my rescue. I had fixed **12** and **99** in mind by the use of the code words for these two numbers, picturing a large *tin pipe* in front of the house. The picture converted into figures gave me **12** and **99.**

Addresses and Other Figures

Addresses, room numbers, catalog figures, bank or business statistics, price lists—any and all kinds of figures—can be fixed in mind by the number code.

A member of one of our New York classes said that he had tried repeatedly to carry in mind the address **634 West 167th Street.** It was the home of a friend in the *restaurant business.*

LESSON FIVE

This suggested *hat check* as an appropriate reminder for **167**, since *hat checks* are a feature of most restaurants *Hat* is **1**, *check* is **67**.

634 is represented by the words *show* **6**, *him* **3**, *your* **4**.

The combination *show him your hat check* designates **634** —**167th Street.** Nothing was necessary to remind him of West, as that part of the address was clear to him.

Room Numbers

The method for room numbers is the same as that used in remembering phone numbers and addresses. The numbers are converted into words, and these are associated with the places.

The following associations were used by a member of one of my classes to remember the name of the occupant and the room number.

Mr. *Herring*—room number **860**.

860 was converted into the word *fishes*. The association between *herring* and *fishes*, once thoroughly impressed, is readily retained.

Mr. *Childe*—room number **912**.

912 was represented by the word *beaten*. Association: A *child* is sometimes *beaten*.

Mr. *Carey*—room number **841**.

841 was transposed into the name *Ford*. Suggestion: A *Ford* will *carry* you anywhere.

Additional Use of Pigeonhole Principle

Lesson Two gave us an insight into the use of our code words for remembering errands, the points of a speech, sales talks, business engagements, and any items of importance.

In addition to enabling us to remember these details, the method creates a mental habit which is beneficial.

It also instils a spirit of enjoyment into what might otherwise be drudgery, and gives us a new hold on many things difficult to retain.

Code Words Create Power

Our code words, as we have seen, fix numbers in mind. They also enable us to do amazing feats—things far beyond the average mind. These can be accomplished only through the use of the code.

There is no limit to the startling things you can do. Then, in addition to the entertainment feature, there is the more important one of mental growth. You are improving while at play—combining entertainment and improvement.

You will see the wonderful power you possess, when once you know your code words, and can interchange the word and its number.

Know Your Code Words

By this time you should know the words *Hat to Daisies* as you know your *A B C's*. You will find them equally useful as long as you live and think.

Lesson Five

Every code word must be identified with its corresponding number. It should instantly suggest the number it represents. Every number should also immediately recall the corresponding word.

A Striking Feat

If you know your code words you can now perform a seemingly impossible feat. After having heard but once a list of numbered items you can instantly assign all items to their proper places, and recall them at will.

Suppose some one were to read to you the following twenty numbered words:

Twenty Items To Be Remembered

1—Snow	8—Carpet	15—Clock
2—Apple	9—Marble	16—Book
3—Pencil	10—Bank	17—Desk
4—Table	11—Barrel	18—Chair
5—Auto	12—Melon	19—Paste
6—Flour	13—Boy	20—Lamp
7—Strap	14—Paint	

You now have twenty items, every one bearing a number, to file away. You do this easily by using your mental pigeonholes—the code words, as explained below. You can also recall these items at will.

First Twenty Code Words

1—Hat	4—Hare	7—Cow
2—Hen	5—Hill	8—Hive
3—Ham	6—Shoe	9—Ape

10—Woods	14—Tire	18—Dove
11—Tide	15—Hotel	19—Tub
12—Tin	16—Dish	20—Nose
13—Team	17—Dog	

You will now file the twenty items by forming a picture association of every one with its corresponding *pigeonhole*.

1—*Snow* is associated with **Hat**. Picture a **Hat** full of *Snow*, or the **Hat** rolling in the *Snow*.

2—*Apple* is associated with **Hen**. It is now easy for you to form such a picture.

3—*Pencil* is pictured with **Ham**. See a *Pencil* sticking in a **Ham**.

4—*Table* is combined with **Hare**. See the **Hare** in your *mind's* eye jumping on a *Table*.

Now go through the list. Form these picture combinations:

1—**Hat**	and *Snow*	11—**Tide**	and *Barrel*
2—**Hen**	and *Apple*	12—**Tin**	and *Melon*
3—**Ham**	and *Pencil*	13—**Team**	and *Boy*
4—**Hare**	and *Table*	14—**Tire**	and *Paint*
5—**Hill**	and *Auto*	15—**Hotel**	and *Clock*
6—**Shoe**	and *Flour*	16—**Dish**	and *Book*
7—**Cow**	and *Strap*	17—**Dog**	and *Desk*
8—**Hive**	and *Carpet*	18—**Dove**	and *Chair*
9—**Ape**	and *Marble*	19—**Tub**	and *Paste*
10—**Woods**	and *Bank*	20—**Nose**	and *Lamp*

Make *clear* pictures. Imagine as much *motion* in them as possible. *Exaggerate* the small objects. See a huge **Tire**, as frequently depicted in advertisements, and see

Lesson Five 187

the *Paint* splashing on the Tire. Make your pictures unusual. Put *color* into your pictures whenever possible.

You Can Now Recall Every Item

Code word number **1, Hat,** recalls our picture—a **Hat** full of *Snow*.

Code word number **2, Hen,** brings back the picture of the **Hen** pecking at the *Apple*.

Code word number **3, Ham,** suggests the big *Pencil* stuck in the **Ham**.

Code word number **4, Hare,** recalls the *Table*.

Code word number **5, Hill,** the *Auto*.

You can go right through your list of code words, and, if you made your picture *clear* and *vivid*, every one, in turn, will recall the corresponding object associated with it.

Form Vivid Pictures

If you miss any words, it may be because you have merely *thought* of the two ideas, but have failed actually to see in your *mind's eye* the *picture combining them,* or because you have failed to imagine *motion, color,* or *exaggeration* in your pictures, as instructed in Lesson One.

This May Surprise You

You can do more than this. You can recall instantly the items by number. For example: What word is opposite number 8?

Code word number 8 is **Hive**. This immediately calls up your picture of a *Carpet* covering a **Hive**, or whatever picture you may have formed of **Hive** and *Carpet*. So you know with certainty that the eighth word is *Carpet*.

Now to recall, say the word opposite number 15. Your fifteenth code word is **Hotel**. This will suggest your picture, **Hotel**—*Clock;* therefore *Clock* is opposite number **15**.

Now suppose you wish to know where *Bank* is located. You will recall your picture of the *Bank* and the **Woods** —**Woods** is the tenth code word—so *Bank* is item number **10**.

Paste recalls **Tub**—code word number 19—therefore *Paste* is the nineteenth item.

In this same way you can recall the word opposite every number, or tell the number if the word is mentioned.

Take More Tests Like This

If, at first, you failed with more than one or two items, taken *ten* at a time until you can recall them without error. Then increase the number to *fifteen,* to *twenty,* or to as many as you wish.

You can do this alone, but it is helpful to have some one call lists to you. In a day or two astonish your friends—combine entertainment with profitable drill.

You will also find that it is not necessary to hear the words in regular order.

Suppose first you had been told number **9** is *Marble*. You need merely recall your ninth code word, **Ape,** and picture **Ape** and the *Marble*.

Then, if the next item given you were number 16, *Book*—code word number **16** is **Dish**—see the **Dish** and the *Book* together in your *mind's eye* in a clear picture.

In your next test, have the words given to you at random instead of in regular order, and as every numbered word is given to you, recall your code word for that number, and form a composite picture of the object and the code word.

Practice with this method every day, taking a new list of objects every time. A few minutes regularly devoted to these exercises will mean quick improvement. Tests such as these are the best kind of memory tonic.

Which Is Easier?

I know that not one normal mind in a thousand can retain figures with the same *ease* and *certainty* as that of my students. But occasionally some beginner who has not learned the code will express the thought that he can remember figures just as readily without the code.

The answer is best given by comparing the number code with shorthand. The beginner can write longhand far more readily than shorthand. If a few words only are to be recorded, he can write them in longhand, but if given dictation at the ordinary rate he is lost until he masters shorthand.

To carry out the comparison, if you have a few numbers to remember it will perhaps be easy for you to do this without the code. But few people can remember a mass of figures with accuracy.

Figure Shorthand

The number code will enable you to retain and recall any amount of figures with certainty. A little regular practice on this *Figure Shorthand* will make you a master of this subject which is both important and fascinating.

Many applications of the number code are given in Lesson Seven. You will find them interesting and practical.

LESSON FIVE

SUMMARY

1—Figure analysis or relationship.

2—Well known figures.

3—Ingenious methods.

4—The number code—a universal method.

5—Numbers remembered by the pictures they represent.

6—*A, e, i, o, u, w, h, y* never have a figure value.

7—All other letters represent figures. You must know their value.

8—Silent letters lose their figure value.

9—One hundred pictorial code words represent numbers 1 to 100. You must know them.

10—Two ways of recording larger numbers:
    a. Combining the code words.
    b. Combining the code letters.

11—Phone numbers, addresses, and other figures.

12—Additional use of pigeonhole plan.

13—The twenty-word test—a striking feat. Tests like this sharpen all your faculties.

14—Practice only is needed—do your share.

15—The number code as practical and as valuable as shorthand.

PRACTICE CHART 5

Write the numbers represented by the letters			Write the letters representing the numbers		
T____	S____	G *Soft*____	1____	4____	9____
N____	B____	K____	3____	5____	6____
M____	L____	SH____	8____	2____	7____
R____	J____	P____	3____	9____	1____
V____	N____	SH____	8____	4____	6____
K____	J____	CH *Hard*____	3____	5____	0____
J____	F____	C *Soft*____	4____	2____	1____
P____	B____	G *Hard*____	8____	3____	6____
N____	P____	L____	2____	4____	8____
S____	O____	CH *Soft*____	7____	3____	9____
K____	T____	M____	1____	5____	6____
T____	M____	SH____	8____	3____	2____
M____	R____	G *Hard*____	4____	8____	7____
D____	N____	C *Hard*____	3____	5____	9____
F____	S____	F____	1____	4____	6____
S____	D____	B____	2____	8____	7____
R____	P____	K____	3____	9____	6____
T____	K____	CH *Hard*____	1____	3____	2____
P____	R____	G *Soft*____	3____	8____	1____
O____	T____	J____	5____	8____	6____
Z____	D____	K____	3____	4____	7____
F____	P____	R____	2____	9____	3____
C____	J____	C *Soft*____	5____	8____	6____
T____	V____	B____	1____	9____	5____
L____	R____	C *Hard*____	2____	8____	7____

PRACTICE CHART 6

Cross out the silent letters, vowels and letters which have no figure value in the following words. Write the figure value of the remaining consonants.

HEN____HARE____PIPE____WOODS____
COW____TIDE____LAKE____HOTEL____
DOG____HIVE____DISH____GNOME____
TUB____DOVE____BOAT____MOOSE____
NUN____NAIL____FIRE____ROACH____
INK____KNOB____CAKE____MATCH____
MUD____MOON____BEAR____LIGHT____
MOP____RAIN____TIRE____CHAIN____
RAT____LACE____LION____GOOSE____
RAM____LILY____FOOT____SHEET____
LAP____JAIL____BELL____SNARE____
JAM____SHIP____COMB____LODGE____
CAN____KITE____LIME____JUDGE____
CAR____CAGE____COAL____CHIEF____
CAB____VASE____FILE____CHAIR____
FAN____FOAM____LAIR____CHECK____
FIG____BOMB____RAKE____HINGE____
FOB____BEEF____NOSE____KNIFE____
BUS____CUFF____TEAM____MUMMY____
BAG____FISH____HILL____CHEESE____
HAT____MUFF____NOSE____WINDOW____
APE____ROOF____LOAF____HAMMER____
HAM____BUSH____RAIL____DAISIES____
TIN____FIFE____SHOE____WARRIOR____
MULE____ROPE____PIANO____HAMMOCK____

PRACTICE CHART 7

Change the following numbers into code word combinations:

1474_____	4731_____
3252_____	4668_____
5179_____	6794_____
2545_____	5689_____
7240_____	9562_____
7128_____	8591_____
9615_____	3442_____
8166_____	9267_____
4541_____	8614_____
6971_____	3684_____

Now translate the following numbers into a single word, or word combinations:

915_____	641_____
324_____	601_____
921_____	215_____
301_____	481_____
814_____	643_____
685_____	700_____
951_____	841_____
514_____	764_____
914_____	264_____
314_____	874_____

LESSON SIX

How to Remember Spelling

Do You "Spell by Ear"?

A teacher, after laboring with Johnny, asked in disgust, "Johnny, how in the world do you spell?"

"Well," pondered Johnny, "I guess I spell just the same as sister plays the piano—by ear."

And the boy, without knowing it, hit the bull's-eye of poor spelling.

There are two ways of spelling. One is by ear, and the other is by eye. Ear spelling is uncertain. *Eye spelling is accurate.* Poor spellers are usually ear spellers, more's the pity, because eye spelling is the easier.

English a Composite Language

Those who have a sound knowledge of Latin, Greek, French, German, and the English of Chaucer have little difficulty in spelling English words, for English is built of words coming from all these languages.

Some modern instructors teach children to spell by *eye* —by visualizing the words—but many pupils persist in spelling as they hear the words. And because they often hear words mispronounced they misspell them.

This becomes a habit, which, in after years, leads to embarrassment and regret. People of excellent education and address are often placed in awkward positions because of some miserable mistake in spelling.

Begin Today to Spell by Eye

Spelling by eye—and by that I mean—by both the real eye and the *mind's eye,* visualization—does not mean that you must discard every habit you have formed of spelling by the sounds of words. Many words are spelled exactly as they sound.

Every one who is not a "good speller" has some pet spelling mistakes that he always makes. Words are learned over and over again, only to be misspelled the next time. And there are new and unfamiliar words cropping up all the time that give trouble.

The Trained Mind's Eye

Troublesome words can be mastered through visualization. Train your *mind's eye* to see the word so clearly that your hand can write it or your lips can spell it.

To read a word carefully and study the letters as they appear in the proper sequence will fix that word in your mind. It will stand out like chalk marks on a blackboard when you need to use it.

When you find certain letters of words are troublesome, make use of exaggeration. Write the words properly and exaggerate the letters causing difficulty. Make them much larger than the rest of the letters in the word.

I give a few illustrations that will show how to proceed with many other words that bother you from time to time.

Privilege

For example, take the word *privilege,* often incorrectly spelled priv*e*lege. Write the word correctly and enlarge the i. Form the visual picture of the word spelled this way:

Priv-I-lege.

Later you will find the picture of the word, formed with the exaggerated *I,* will come back to your mind and give you the correct spelling.

Writing priv-I-lege in this manner a few times fixes *I* as the central letter. Note that there are four letters before and four after *I*. This will prevent the mistake of spelling it priv*e*lege.

Until

It may be a question of a single or double letter; for example, the word *until*. Write it unti*ll,* and then mark a large X through the final *L,* thus:

UNTIL̶X̶

I have been surprised at the large number of well educated people who spell *develop* with a final e, as develop*e.*

This is due no doubt to confusion with the word *envelope.*

To impress the correct spelling of develop, add a large capital E, thus:

DevelopE.

Then cross out the E as you did with the second L in untilL.

Use this plan if words of this character trouble you.

Visualize Words—and They Will Stick

Print the troublesome word instead of writing it. Enlarge the letters that cause the trouble. Better still, print these particular letters in a different color by using crayon pencils. Impress the word thus written by gazing at it a moment. Shut your eyes and see in your *mind's eye* the word thus altered.

A little ingenuity in studying words will make you a good speller. Students who considered themselves hopeless spellers have made wonderful strides by using such methods.

Some Stumbling-Blocks

A common stumbling-block is the use of *i* and *e,* in words such as niece, friend, receive, etc.

You can master these words. Remember this:

Ei always follows the letter *c:*

| Ceiling | Conceive | Deceive | Receipt |
| Conceit | Deceit | Perceive | Receive |

Ie usually follows the other letters:

Believe	Chief	Niece	Siege
Belief	Friend	Piece	Sieve
Brief	Grief	Relief	Thief

Rules in spelling, as a general thing, are not as helpful as are a little care, observation, and the use of visualization. The trouble with all spelling rules is that there are so many exceptions.

Here is one spelling rule that will help you:

I before *E,* except after *C,*
Or when sounded as *A*
As in *neighbor* and *weigh.*

I advise you to pause here a moment if you have trouble with words of this sort. Understand this rule thoroughly.

Lesson Six

Note carefully the above lists. See that *c* is followed by *ei*. Most letters, such as *l, n, p, s,* are followed by *ie* —i before e. *C* is followed by *ei*.

This rule will serve as a guide, although there are a few exceptions.

The words *seize* and *leisure* are exceptions to the rule.

Apply Your Common Sense

The correct spelling of many bothersome words can be fixed firmly in mind by common-sense means.

Stationery and *stationary* are trouble makers. Just remember that a *stationer* sells station*e*ry. This suggests the *e*.

You recall this easily. It will serve as a guide to the spelling of the other word, of the same sound, station*a*ry, meaning fixed, immovable.

Busy or Buisy?

Busy is occasionally spelled bu*i*sy or bus*ey*. Just think of it as a *busy* word, with no time to put in any extra letters. Write it a few times with this thought in mind.

Words like *necessity* and *recollect* can be conquered if we pronounce them in practice, as *ne-cessity* and *re-collect*. The division of the word into syllables will impress the single *c*.

Recommend

I never have any trouble with the word *recommend*. I have formed the habit of separating it into syllables, and as I write it, pronounce it *re-commend*.

This plan is a most effective aid to good spelling. You can use it frequently.

If you fix the correct spelling of *necessity* in mind, *necessary* can be linked with it.

Repetition

Repetition is also a puzzler—it is frequently misspelled rep*i*tition. Associate *repetition* with *repeat*. There is no danger of spelling rep*e*at rep*i*at. When you fix clearly in mind the similarity between *repe*at and *repe*tition, your trouble is ended.

Piece, a word that troubles many, can be associated with a *piece of pie*. This will solve the problem, since *pie* represents the first three letters of *piece*.

There are many bothersome words that are overcome by making a striking appeal to the *mind's eye*.

For example, *expense* is spelled expen*c*e by many persons, probably because of their familiarity with *fence, defence,* etc.

Here is a simple, sure and practical way to fix the correct spelling in mind:

Expense is usually a matter of dollars and cents. Therefore, write or print the word in the following manner:

EXPEN$E

Merely enlarging the S is also effective.

expenSe

Gauge is one of the most tantalizing words in the dictionary, and it is fortunate that we do not meet it frequently. It is usually spelled incorrectly.

To fix this word in mind, should it be one of your trouble-makers, impress it on your *mind's eye* in this way:

ga U ge

Distinctly see this large U as the *middle* letter. Write the word in this manner once or twice every day for a few days. Do this with all words that trouble you.

Separate is often incorrectly spelled sep-*e*-rate. Correct the bad habit by writing the word

sep A rate

Think of the capital *A* as a large wedge that separates the word into two parts.

It is important to persist in this practice for a few days. This makes lasting impressions. *Be systematic. Keep a list, and add other words as they present themselves.* Review this list occasionally, applying the various principles outlined in this lesson.

Judgment

Many are prone to put an extra *e* in *judgment* and spell it judg*e*ment. In this case insert a large capital *E* and cross it out. Make the *E* as large as possible.

Impressing the wrong letter upon the mind may not be as proper as emphasizing the right one, but it is effective.

A common tendency is to omit *d* in knowledge. Here it is advisable to write the capital *D* very large. Do this a few times.

The combination of *dg* in ju*dg*ment can also be impressed upon most minds by putting a circle around these two letters.

Separating a word that troubles you into syllables is frequently all that is necessary to photograph the proper outlines upon the mind. For example:

    Ac-com-mo-date   Ab-bre-vi-ate
    Re-com-mend   A-mend

Words Ending in -ant and -ent

Few words give more trouble than those ending in *ant* and *ent*. Upon these, at times, the most expert spellers will trip.

They sometimes spell abund*a*nt abund*e*nt; consist*e*nt consist*a*nt, and so on. These words yield to simple treatment.

First, take the words having the suffix *ant,* such as the following:

Abundant	Assistant	Defendant
Accountant	Attendant	Observant
Arrogant	Clairvoyant	Recreant
Assailant	Combatant	Repentant

Write every word several times with the large *A* as:

    abundAnt

Underlining the *a* will also make a strong impression on the *mind's eye*.

Any one of these methods will serve to place the word in your mind permanently, *if you will do your part*. Your part is to write your words daily for two or three days, in accordance with the instruction given.

Practice—do not be satisfied with *reading* the words.

Belligerent

In the case of words ending with *ent,* use a similar method. Take, as an example, the word *belligerent.*

Write the word in the usual way, except in the case of the *E,* which you should make extraordinarily large—belligerEnt. Use a script *E*. Make a big capital *E* that will stand out with sufficient prominence to compel your attention.

Work out the following list of words having the suffix *ent* as directed:

Confident	Equivalent	Penitent
Consistent	Excellent	Persistent
Convalescent	Independent	Precedent
Correspondent	Insistent	Superintendent

Other Troublesome Words

Other words that cause trouble, because of the sound *A,* are the following:

Accessible	Impossible	Possible
Audible	Indelible	Responsible
Contemptible	Indigestible	Sensible
Eligible	Inexhaustible	Susceptible
Forcible	Perceptible	Terrible
Horrible	Plausible	Visible

You will find all that is necessary to impress such words correctly is to dot the letter *I* with an extraordinarily large dot, as:

Possible

Run through this list four or five times. Add other

words with which you have difficulty. Write every word, and dot the *I* as has been suggested.

Make the letter that causes the trouble stand out clearly and give an account of itself.

Double Letters

To fix double letters in mind, the best method is to underscore the letters doubled.

Here, for instance, is the word *abbreviate.*

Underscore the double *b* with two lines, and after it, in parenthesis, write (2 b's) in this fashion:

ABBREVIATE (2 b's)

The word *accommodate* has two sets of double letters. Write it this way:

ACCOMMODATE (AC-COM-MODATE)

Pronounce the word, separated into syllables, every time you write it. Sound every letter. Say ac-com-mo-date.

In *committee* there are three sets of double letters:

CO MM I TT EE

Fix the word in your mind thus:

C O MM I TT EE
(2 m's, 2 t's, 2 e's)

Words Ending in f or fe

Still another class of troublesome words are those ending in *f* or *fe,* which, upon extending to the plural, drop the *f* or *fe* and take *ves*. Of this class the following are examples:

Knife......Knives		Shelf......Shelves	
Leaf.......Leaves		Thief.....Thieves	
Life.......Lives		Wife......Wives	
Loaf.......Loaves		Wolf......Wolves	

Thoroughly impress these plurals upon the memory—write them with the last three letters of the plural enlarged, and in heavily printed forms, as:

      liVES   kniVES

All as a Prefix

The use of the word *all* as a prefix often adds to the difficulty of spelling.

When *all* is combined with another word as a prefix, the final *l* is dropped, as you will observe in the following list. STUDY this list, and write it several times:

Almighty	Although
Almost	Altogether
Already	Always

Note *all right* is not a single word, and is therefore written with double *ll*.

Well as a Prefix

The same rule applies to words in which *well* is used as a prefix, and to words in which *full* is used as a suffix, as follows:

Welcome	Beautiful	Peaceful
Welfare	Hateful	Woeful

Apply to the foregoing lists any of the means thus far given that are most resultful.

Words Ending with Y

Such words as cry, try, etc., ending in *y*, often confuse even accurate spellers when they desire to add *ing*. They are uncertain when they should retain or reject the *y*.

Write this list a few times, making a large, heavy *Y*:

Carry....CarrYing   Hurry....HurrYing
Cry.....CrYing   Pity.....PitYing
Envy....EnvYing   Study....StudYing
Fry......FrYing   Try......TrYing

In short, it is important to remember that words ending in *y*, preceded by a consonant, retain the *y* when *ing* is added.

But when *ed* is added, instead of *ing*, the *y* is changed to *i*.

Practice on the following list, separating the *I* by hyphens on either side. Forming the *I* with a blue or red pencil will assist the memory and make keener impressions.

Carry....Carr-I-ed   Hurry....Hurr-I-ed
Cry.....Cr-I-ed   Pity.....Pit-I-ed
Envy....Env-I-ed   Study....Stud-I-ed
Fry......Fr-I-ed   Try......Tr-I-ed

Words Ending in E

Words ending in *e*, preceded by a consonant, drop the *e* when *ing* is added.

Arrange becomes arranging. Love becomes loving.
Change   "   changing. Make   "   making.

Lesson Six

Charge becomes	charging.	Move becomes	moving.
Cure	"	curing.	Observe	"	observing.
Deceive	"	deceiving.	Place	"	placing.
Divide	"	dividing.	Plunge	"	plunging.
Freeze	"	freezing.	Rule	"	ruling.
Give	"	giving.	Smoke	"	smoking.
Have	"	having.	Take	'	taking.
Hope	"	hoping.	Use	"	using.
Improve	"	improving.	Wade	"	wading.
Lose	"	losing	Write	"	writing.

To emphasize these changes the student may write the words as follows:

Hop E ing   Writ E ing   Charg E ing

striking out with a cross the superfluous *E* in the manner shown. If you can get along without these negative ideas, do so.

The examples given, and other words of the same class, should be written daily for a time until you are familiar with them. Use the means you find best suited to fix the correct spelling in mind.

Words Ending with a Single Consonant

One class of words in everyday use, and of much importance, consists of verbs ending with a single consonant, preceded by a single vowel. With these many have difficulty:

Run, Forget, Whip, etc.

In carrying such words into their secondary form— or, to state the matter differently, in converting them into present participles—we must double the final consonant, thus:

Forget—F o r g e t t i n g   Run—R u n n i n g

Many of us fail to follow this rule, and, as a result, inexcusably misspell a very simple word.

In carrying such words into their third, or past participle form, the same rule applies, as:

Beg—B e g g i n g—b e g g e d
Slip—s l i p p i n g—s l i p p e d

Below are several examples of verbs of this class. Write this list daily for a few days.

The rule, simply expressed, is: In adding *ing* or *ed* to verbs ending with *one* consonant preceded by a vowel, *double* the consonant. Thus:

Cut.........Cut ting
Forget......Forget ting
Get.........Get ting
Let.........Let ting
Run.........Run ning
Blur........Blur ring.......Blur red
Commit......Commit ting....Commit ted
Drop........Drop ping......Drop ped
Knit........Knit ting......Knit ted
Refer.......Refer ring.....Refer red
Stir........Stir ring......Stir red
Wrap........Wrap ping......Wrap ped

To illustrate the rule further, take the words *pat* and *part*. Pat is a single syllable word ending in a *single* consonant preceded by a *single* vowel. It consequently is extended by doubling the final consonant, and becomes *p a t t i n g*.

The word *part* ends with two consonants and, therefore is outside the rule given. To extend it, it becomes *p a r t i n g*.

Accent Indicates Spelling

In some words the *accent* indicates when the spelling is to be changed.

Of such words are *prefer* and *refer*.

In both of these you will note that the accent is upon the last syllable. The same is true of *preferred* and *referred*.

In spelling *preference* or *reference*, the accent changes to the first syllable.

When this is the case the rule is to *drop one of the r's*, with the result that we have *preference, reference*.

Work out for yourself a list of words of this kind. For that matter, it is advisable throughout this lesson to use your own mind, and your own initiative in every possible way.

Practice on Troublesome Words

Do not rest satisfied with the lists given here. They are not intended to cover every word in the vocabulary to which the methods I have given you can be made to apply. They are given merely as examples of several sorts of words employed and of the methods applicable to them.

Study to improve your spelling. Make additional lists of your own. Use the dictionary for the correct spelling of any word of which you are uncertain. At the same time learn the meaning of the word.

The dictionary, if properly used, provides an education.

Keep a list of your words, and review them from time to time.

How to Remember History, Science, Law, and Other Subjects

The natural tendency of the mind is to associate and to compare. Nearly everything that occurs in our life reminds us of something else. This is the unconscious exercise of the associative faculty, so essential to good memory.

It is this fact that makes memory improvement possible. Training of the memory is guiding and directing the associative power along correct lines.

The person who realizes the resources of his mind and the value of memory instinctively seeks the thing that will fix the incident in mind.

Helpful Hints

I shall now give you a few hints that will prove helpful. Every one of them represents a large class of memory problems. Adapt them to your needs as they arise and you will soon prove their value.

I have previously indicated how easily the nautical term *port* is associated with *left,* because the words contain the same number of letters. The color of port wine fixes in mind the red color of the port light.

Simple means like these will aid you in solving many

vexing problems of memory. Be on the lookout at all times for such helps.

Often a little hint from the instructor will be of help in overcoming difficulties.

A Practical Suggestion

Some high-school students were perplexed in trying to remember that *amylose* is a product of digested starch.

The teacher finally suggested:

Amy loses her corn*starch* pudding.

In this manner *amylose* and *starch* were indelibly linked in the students' minds.

The distinction between *chyme* and *chyle* is hard to remember.

Chyme is the result of digestion in the stomach. You will observe that chyMe and stoMach each contain the letter M.

Having thus associated chyme and stomach it will be easy to remember that *chyle* is formed in the intestines.

The *tricuspid* valve is on the *right* side of the heart. The suggestion—*try* (tri) to do *right*—fixes the proper location—the *right* side.

Noteworthy Coincidences

Franklin Pierce was our *Fourteenth President*. Note that the initials *F. P.* stand for both Franklin Pierce and Fourteenth President. Note also that there are *fourteen* letters in the name Franklin Pierce.

He was elected in 1852, or '52. This is an easy date to remember because there are 52 weeks in the year.

When Abraham Lincoln was elected the first time, Hamlin was chosen Vice-President.

Observe that the name *Abraham Lincoln* contains, in regular order, the letters forming the name *Hamlin:*

>AbraHAM-LINcoln

Increased use of observation will suggest many ways in which facts worth remembering can be stored away.

Initialing

Initialing is an orderly arrangement of the first letters of words or points we wish to carry in mind. Facts arranged in this way are recalled readily.

The first letter is the prominent feature of a word. It is the one that becomes the most clearly imprinted in the mind. Given this first letter we can usually recall the entire word.

I had occasion to communicate with the following men:

>Sisson
>Merrill
>Ireland
>Lennon
>Eaton

Arranged in the above order, the first letters formed:

>S-M-I-L-E

This gave me an easy and sure way to keep these five names in mind.

This is an interesting and valuable principle. You can apply it indefinitely. It is especially useful to the student and has a wide application in business and social life.

You can use initialing for your business engagements, home errands, recalling locations, streets, and points of interest, legal, medical, and other scientific terms, and the personnel of corporation, company, or gathering.

Schoolroom Suggestions

I have met many people who attribute their good memories entirely to the practical suggestions received in the schoolroom.

Perhaps you were taught the colors of the rainbow through initialing. These colors may be impressed upon the mind by the use of the coined word:

VIBGYOR

This is an odd word but one easily and lastingly fixed in the mind. It gives the key to the colors:

V—Violet
I —Indigo
B—Blue
G—Green
Y—Yellow
O—Orange
R—Red

Many music teachers use initialing with success. They tell you that the notes in the spaces spell:

F-A-C-E

They also use another method of initialing for remembering the line notes—E, G, B, D, F.

Every one of these letters is used as an initial letter of a word. These words are then formed into the following sentence:

Every Good Boy Deserves Favors

Two other sentences that serve to recall the notes G, D, A, E, B, F, and illustrate the method, are:

*G*o *D*own *A*nd *E*at *B*lue *F*ish
and
*G*ood *D*ogs *A*ll *E*at *B*ad *F*ood

A little ingenuity in initialing creates an added interest in studies. At the same time it affords an easy way to learn many difficult subjects.

Most of us remember the order of the planets—Mercury, Venus, Earth, Mars, and Jupiter.

There are three other planets that frequently give us trouble to remember—Saturn, Uranus, and Neptune.

This difficulty is overcome by noting that the initials of these three planets spell SUN:

S—Saturn
U—Uranus
N—Neptune

The cabinet of Charles II, King of England, affords a good example of the value of initialing in remembering historical data.

The five men composing the cabinet of King Charles were:

C—Clifford
A—Arlington
B—Buckingham
A—Ashley
L—Lauderdale

You will note the first letters taken in regular order form the word:

CABAL

This was evidently a most appropriate word to apply to that distinguished coterie, since *cabal* means a group of persons brought together to intrigue or conspire.

In the study or practice of law initialing will prove of value.

At one time a young student was troubled by the phrase:

*M*inerals *U*nder *T*he *S*urface

He was engaged in compiling references and data to be used in mining litigation. He could not remember the exact wording of the phrase until he observed that the first letters spelled:

M U T S
M—Minerals
U —Under
T —The
S —Surface

Initialing applies, in a practical way, to the study of the old English law. The items that follow can be mastered in their order by law students.

The Twelve Principal Methods by Which Title to Things Personal Can Be Acquired or Lost

A—Administration S—Succession
B—Bankruptcy O—Occupancy
C—Contract F—Forfeiture
G—Gift or Grant T—Testament
M—Marriage J—Judgment
C—Custom P—Prerogative

Accepted merely as letters, these initials have no special significance. If we use a little ingenuity we can readily tie them together into a group of words that will remain in the memory.

J P is the abbreviation for Justice of the Peace. The letters M, C, S, O, F, T suggest the surname MC SOFT. Let us consider MC SOFT a Justice of the Peace. Then add the initials A, B, C, G and we have

A. B. C. G. MC SOFT—J. P.

In your *mind's eye,* picture that name appearing upon a courtroom door.

A. B. C. G. McSoft, J. P.

Now I do not say that all you have to do is to read this list once or twice. It is necessary, in order to fix this grouping in mind to review the process a number of times.

Memorizing the list by straight repetition would not require much time, but, on the other hand, it would make such a slight impression that it would be forgotten quickly. Initialing is a definite process by which these and other lists can be fixed in mind permanently.

The Ten Principal Sorts of Incorporeal Hereditaments

C—Commons
O—Offices
W—Ways
A—Annuities
R—Rents
D—Dignities
F—Franchises
A—Advowsons
C—Corrodies or Pensions
T—Tithes

The initial letters, in their order, spell

COWARD—FACT

This can be linked with incorporeal hereditaments by thinking of this *terrible title* as a COWARD-ly FACT.

A certain attorney could not recall the names of the six judges holding court in his city, or the numbers of their respective courtrooms, from 1 to 6.

The names of the judges in the order of their courts, from 1 to 6, were:

K—Kavanaugh
M—Morrow
M—McGinn
D—Davis
G—Gatens
G—Gantenbein

He ingeniously put the initials together, forming this sentence:

Keep Many Men Daily Good Gang

Initialing was used to remember the following difficult name:

    Savings Union Bank and Trust Company

These first letters suggested

        S U B Treasury

The letters S U B served to recall Savings Union Bank which had been a stumbling block before.

Initials as Applied to Anatomy

The doctor and the student of anatomy will find initialing useful. Many students are obliged to use it, particularly in the study of anatomy.

At one time I tested the memory of a number of doctors concerning the order of the twelve pairs of cranial nerves. Every medical student learns them, but I found only a few of the practitioners who had retained them. Those who were able to recall them had originally learned them by initialing.

Cranial Nerves

The cranial nerves in their correct order are:

        O—Olfactory
        O—Optic
        M—Motor Oculi
        P—Pathetic
        T—Trifacial
        A—Abducent
        F—Facial
        A—Auditory

G—Glossopharyngeal
P—Pneumogastric
S—Spinal Accessory
H—Hypoglossal

These first letters, in their proper order, suggest the sentence:

O, O, Mamma! Papa Took A Fork
And Gave Pony Some Hay.

Bones of the Wrist

The bones of the wrist are:

S —Scaphoid
S —Semilunar
C—Cuneiform
P—Pisiform
T—Trapezium
T—Trapezoid
O—Os Magnum
U—Unciform

The first letters suggest the sentence:

Silly Sammy Carelessly Put The Trap Out Unset.

The same plan can be applied effectively to many other terms in anatomy and to facts in other studies.

Chemical and Other Formulae

Engineering, chemical, and other formulae are usually hard to learn. The student should at all times exercise his visual memory to impress the appearance of the desired formulae upon the *mind's eye*.

A young student in chemistry, whose memory was excellent in most respects, found it impossible to recall chemical formulae. He had much trouble with one in particular:

$$4H\ P\ O_3.$$

I stimulated his imagination by suggesting to him a certain picture. It astonished him. It was entirely new, and a radical departure for him. With astonishing success he applied the method I outlined. He substituted for the formula this sentence:

$$4\text{ High Priests, O! O! O!}$$

The letters H, P, O, signified nothing, except hydrogen, phosphorus, and oxygen, which, to this beginner in chemistry, meant little. Combined into words as above they conveyed the impression of life and action. By such emphasis the memory can retain them.

Of course, the process was out of the ordinary, but it served the purpose.

I do not urge the use of unusual methods when simple means will answer. As long as the method serves the purpose it is good.

The following are a number of ways by which students have obtained good results:

The formula for *Apatite* is
$$Ca\ (FCl)_2\ 3(Ca_3\ (PO_4)_2)$$

One of my students of ingenious imagination remembered this by:

Calves 2 Ate 3 Cabbages Thrice (while) Poor Ox Foraged (4-aged) Twice

As analyzed:

$Ca(FCl)_2$—Calves Two
$3(Ca_3)$—3 Cabbages Thrice
$(PO4)_2$—Poor Ox Foraged (4-aged) Twice

The formula for *Cryolite* is

$Na_3 AlF_6$

This suggested a little boy who had been lost. Searchers found him at length *crying* beside a *light* (cryalite). They asked him if he knew the way home and he replied:

"Nay, Nay, Nay." (Na_3)

His name was ALF and he was 6 years old (AlF_6). *Absurd?* Certainly—but *effective!*

When you have once mastered this method you will find these examples will not compare with those you will invent for yourself, if your memory *needs* such aids.

Help for Students of Pharmacy.

Initialing can be used to fix troublesome combinations in mind. I will give a single illustration:

Tincture Guaiaci Ammoniata, compounded of Alcohol, oil of Lemon, Ammonia and oil of Nutmeg suggested

Al Lemons A Nut.

The formula for Horsepower spells

PLAN

*P*ressure, *L*ength, *A*rea, *N*umber of Revolutions.

Presidents of the United States

It is a remarkable fact that very few American citizens can repeat correctly the names of our Presidents.

We learned them in our school days by repetition, and, as a consequence, have forgotten them.

As a matter of pride we should all be familiar with the names. Through the use of the visual or initial method we can learn them quickly.

The following are the names of the Presidents, and the key words by which they can be remembered:

The names appear in heavy type, and the lines in light-face type furnish the story or jingle:

Washington	**Adams**	**Jefferson**	**Madison**
Washington	And	Jefferson	Made
Monroe	**Adams**	**Jackson**	**Van Buren**
Many	A	Joke.	Van Buren
Harrison	**Tyler**	**Polk**	**Taylor**
Had	Troubles	Plenty	To
Fillmore	**Pierce**	**Buchanan**	**Lincoln**
Find	Poor	Bugles.	Link
Johnson	**Grant**	**Hayes**	**Garfield**
Johnson	Gave	Hayes	General
Arthur	**Cleveland**	**Harrison**	**Cleveland**
Arthur's	Cigar.	He	Cleared
McKinley	**Roosevelt**	**Taft**	**Wilson**
McKinley's	Road	To	Washington.

Similar stories can be formed to carry other lists in mind. The practice is beneficial.

Application is essential.

Merely reading and understanding these methods and lists is not sufficient in order to master them.

How to Remember Foreign Vocabularies

In Lesson Three you were shown how an unfamiliar name, such as *Harnecker,* can be recalled by associating it with a familiar idea such as *arnica.* We describe this process by saying *arnica* is a *reminder* for *Harnecker.*

This same principle of *reminders* is applied to advantage in learning foreign words. Many of these, like names of people, are entirely unfamiliar. By comparing them with words that are familiar, and that serve as *reminders* for them, we are applying the principle on which memory is founded.

The student familiar with several languages can trace the derivations of words and acquire other languages in a scientific way.

The majority, who must depend upon their knowledge of English, may learn foreign words easily and permanently by using *reminders* for troublesome words.

Connecting Links

These *reminders* serve as connecting links between the English and the foreign words. They remind us of the foreign words because of similarity in sound. The following words scarcely require explanation, but let us take the first word—*amusing.*

This reminds us of *diverting,* which, in turn, reminds us of the similar sounding word *divertido.*

Several years ago I noted that the Spanish word for

Ends is *Acaba*

The thought occurred to me that at the end of every car line there is a car barn. *A car barn is similar in* sound to *Acaba*.

Now, if I wish to recall the Spanish word for *ends*, I recall the thought associated with the *end* of the line—*a car barn—acaba*. The process is instantaneous.

The student usually learns foreign words by laborious repetition. Note the saving of time in learning the following Spanish words:

English	*Reminder*	*Spanish*
Amusing	Diverting	Divertido
Alone	Solitude	Solo
Ancient	Antique	Antiguo
Car	Coach	Coche
Change	Mutation	Mudar
Church	Ecclesiastic	Iglesia
Compel	Oblige	Obligar
Cold	Frigid	Frio
Dark	Obscure	Oscuro
Door	Portal	Puerto
Drink	Imbibe	Beber
Easy	Facility	Facil
Ends	A car barn	Acaba
Finger	Digit	Dedo
Follow	Sequence	Seguir
Glad	Content	Contento
Go away	Disperse	Irse

English	Reminder	Spanish
High	Altitude	Alto
Keep	Guard	Guardar
Knife	Cut	Cuchillo
Lost	Perished	Perdido
Meat	Carnal	Carne
Mild	Bland	Blando
Printed	Impression	Impreso
Refuse	Negation	Negarse
Raw	Crude	Crudo
Right	Direct	Direcho
Sell	Vend	Vender
Sleep	Dormant	Dormir
Small	Chic	Chico
Teeth	Dentist	Dientes
Thin	Delicate	Delgado
Think	Pensive	Pensar
Wash	Lavatory	Lavar
Wave	Undulate	Onda
Window	Ventilate	Venta
Word	Palaver	Palabra
Written	Secretary	Escrito
Young	Juvenile	Joven

This way of learning a foreign vocabulary makes it interesting, and converts drudgery into pleasant exercise.

Reminders Better Than Repetition

A well known author, who learned eight languages quickly, told me the use of *reminders* was absolutely essential to him. He had no gift for languages but made progress where so many fail, because he used imagination and association instead of depending entirely upon repetition.

A Cumbersome Method

Early writers on memory advocated a chain of *reminders* from one word to another. For example, in proceeding from the English word *spear* to the Latin equivalent *hasta*, the following series of *reminders* is given:

spear—thrust—quick motion—hasty—hasta

This method is awkward and impractical, and has often been cited as an example of memory methods. It illustrates one way of spoiling a good idea by employing it to an unreasonable extent.

Latin Words

The examples of Spanish words given make clear to you how the principle may be applied to the mastery of words in any language. Here are a few illustrations of Latin words:

English	*Reminder*	*Latin*
Crown	Coronation	Corona
Dog	Canine	Canis
Drop	Distill	Stilla
Father	Paternal	Pater
Field	Acre	Ager
Free	Liberate	Liber
Head	Cap	Caput
Horse	Equine	Equus

Lesson Six

English	Reminder	Latin
House	Domicile	Domus
Land	Territory	Terra
Man	Human	Homo
Rob	Rapine	Rapto
Sour	Acid	Acer
Think	Cogitate	Cogito
War	Belligerent	Bellum
Water	Aquatic	Aqua
Writer	Scribe	Scriba

The student of foreign languages usually has trouble with the grammar, especially the declension of nouns and the conjugation of verbs.

Terminations

Learning terminations is usually accomplished only through much repetition.

We cannot go into this subject thoroughly here. I wish merely to point out a few helpful suggestions for fixing terminations in mind.

The Latin endings in the indicative and subjunctive moods, first, second, and third person plural, are:

mus, tis, nt

Many years ago my attention was called to the sentence:

Missed His Aunt

This enabled me to retain these terminations while through disuse many others were forgotten.

In Spanish we meet with the endings

o, a, amos, an.

For example:

>Hablo—I speak.
>Habla—he speaks.
>Hablamos—we speak.
>Hablan—they speak.

Here is how an ingenious student quickly fixed in mind, by means of mental picturing, the endings *o, a, amos, an*. A small boy speaking or politely bowing, saying:

>"*Oh, ah, Amos* and *Ann.*"

as he passes Amos and his girl, Ann.

Use your imagination when you study foreign languages.

For Postal Clerks

The material which postal clerks must learn can be remembered easily by the use of *association* and *visualization*.

Here is an example of these principles as applied by one of my Western students in learning a series of stations, as follows:

Mansfield and Wenatchee Mail Scheme

Howard	Mansfield	Hopewell	St. Germain
Dyer	Waco	Waterville	Allstown
Jameson	Tonkey	Appledale	Palisades
Douglas	Del Rio	Lamoine	Rex
Spenser	Leahy	Farmer	
Nelson	Alameda	Withrow	

He made a story linking the reminders for these stations. Ingenious methods like these can be applied to save time and labor of learning. It makes easy and interesting many an otherwise disagreeable if not hopeless task.

Howdy, James. You remember *Douglas Spencer, Nell's Son*—the one that got on the old *Mansfield—weighs* about a *ton?* He was over last night and said that *Del Rio* and the Chinese cook *Le He* ran off with *Alameda Hopewell* and started from *Waterville* to *Appledale.* But old man *Lamoine* and a farmer named *Withrow* roused the whole country between *St. Germain* and *Allstown,* caught them near the *Palisades* and *wrecked* the whole scheme.

Note that *Howdy* represents *Howard* and *Dyer, Nell's son* designated *Nelson, Ton* stands for *Tonkey, Le He* for *Leahy.*

Here is another illustration by the same student:

North Bend and Seattle Scheme

Edgewick	Preston	Monahan	Hollywood
Tanner	Falls City	Inglewood	Hazelwood
Snoqualmie	High Point	Redmond	Factoria
North Bend	Issaquah	Derby	Kennydale

Ed Wicks, a *tanner,* and I were hunting *Snow Quail* near *North Bend.* A storm came up, so we *Prest on* towards *Falls City.* We came to a *High Point.* I saw a squaw. I put *money in her hand* for *Ingle Wood.* Meantime Ed traded a *Red Man* a *Derby* for some *Holly Wood.* We built a fire where the *Hazelwood Factory* now stands in *Kennydale.*

This student received one of the highest marks in the examinations as a result of using these and other methods of association and visualization in learning his postal routes.

The Mind Must Be Used Properly

Dr. Swain, in "How to Study," says:

> "Important as it is to learn how to study, it is singular that most students do not learn it, and that little effort is made to teach it. It is assumed that children know how to study because they have brains. Probably a large majority of our college students today have not learned how to study properly, and find it difficult or impossible to take up a new study and master it. They have only learned how to do certain routine things in a mechanical way. They have learned by rote."

Every Faculty Should Be Employed

In order to study properly it is necessary to use all the faculties.

Observation, Visualization, Imagination, and the use of logical *associations* create *interest* in any task and develop *concentration.* This means an improved mind and a better memory.

Observation

An old Scotch professor asked his students to observe him closely. He put his finger into a jar containing a vile-smelling chemical, then placed a finger in his mouth. Requesting his students to do what he did, every one of them regretted it for the taste of the liquid was sickening.

The canny professor then explained the mystery of his immunity. "You did not *observe* me closely, for if you had, you would have seen that the finger I put into my mouth was not the same one I put into the jar."

Close observation results in deep impressions. Impressions well recorded are easy of recall, and it is for that reason that most of the treatises on memory devote much space to observation tests and exercises based upon observation.

I do not say that these exercises are not valuable, but they do not reckon with human nature. Few people are so constituted in these days of rush and bustle that they will follow a tedious program.

Concentration

Observation demands concentration and few people really know how to concentrate. Concentration requires attention, which in turn is based upon interest. Therefore observation and concentration result from making things interesting.

My course has been prepared with that point always in view. It is always interesting and easy. Follow it step by step and understandingly and it will furnish you with a new interest in every subject.

A Great Change

One of my students, a prominent architect, said recently, "Killing time never bothers me any more. Formerly, when obliged to wait for a train, minutes seemed like hours. Now hours seem like minutes, because of the many interesting and helpful things I can do in exercising my mind. This course has added years to my life."

Here are a few practical, interesting and resultful tests. They will improve your ability to observe and will repay you well for every moment devoted to them. Make a game of these tests and invite your friends and family to join in the fun.

Picture Test

So far as I know, the following test has never been described before. It is an excellent educator for young and old. Use any drawing or picture large enough for all to see.

Select some one object shown in the picture but do not mention it. Just give the letter which begins the name of the item.

For example, if the item selected is a *rose*, the letter to be mentioned is *r*. The first person giving the correct answer has the privilege of making the next selection.

Children taught observation in this way will use their eyes to far better advantage all through life.

The Observation Test

This test or game can be played in many ways. The most interesting plan is to put about thirty different articles on a table and cover them until the test begins. Any articles you have handy may be used.

The persons taking part in the test are grouped about the table, which is then uncovered. They are given from fifteen to thirty seconds to look at the articles.

Every one is then given paper and pencil and the one listing the most articles from memory is the winner.

A large group is not necessary. Two people can practice this test with profit and enjoyment.

Another good plan is to look briefly at show windows containing a number of items and afterward see how many articles you can name.

The main thing is to develop the faculty of seeing the entire layout clearly in the *mind's eye*.

Map Drawing

Map drawing affords excellent practice for students of memory improvement because it requires close observation. I dare say not one person in thousands can draw from memory a rough outline of the United States.

Drawing an outline of the State in which he lives is usually impossible for the average person, unless he lives in Wyoming or Colorado. This inability is not at all surprising. The eye has not been trained to remember what it sees.

By using a little imagination and some regular practice you will find many interesting things in map drawing that will aid the memory.

For example, the lower portion of the State of Michigan resembles an old hunched-up woman with her hands in a shawl trying to keep warm. Also note the topknot on her head.

Interesting Outlines

The outline of Italy closely resembles a high-heeled boot drawn back to kick a stone out of the way. The stone being the island of Sicily.

With a little imagination the outline of England and Wales may resemble an old man riding a hobby horse.

The continent of South America looks like an elephant's head and trunk.

France, Spain, and Portugal bear a close resemblance to a pig's head with the snout in a bucket.

Drawing lines between the *cities* in the *states* in which you are interested will aid the *mind's eye* in fixing their location as well as the *outline* of the *state*.

By making these outlines a few times you will get deep impressions on the mind and readily develop a geographical memory.

Puzzle Maps

The mind is also aided by the use of puzzle or jigsaw maps. These maps are usually mounted on wood, or heavy cardboard, which is then cut along the state lines. It is good practice to assemble the various states into their proper location.

This makes an excellent game for the children and valuable practice for elders. The maps can be obtained at book, toy, or department stores as a rule, but if you are unable to obtain them locally, specific information will be furnished on request.

Games That Improve the Memory

There are many interesting games which not only improve the memory but are educational and helpful. They are of aid to children and to the entire family.

Parents should give a little attention to this subject. Properly directed effort will make all the difference between a discontented and a happy, well conducted family.

"Idleness is the cause of all mischief." No student of this course needs to be idle. The brain requires change of occupation—not idleness.

The tired business man after a day of intense mental strain will find complete rest and recreation in these lessons.

Spelling Games

I learned this game when a boy and have taught it to people of all ages. It is a most enjoyable and helpful game.

Every one of the party is given paper and pencil. A word is then selected and the person forming the longest list of words made up from the letters of the selected word wins the game.

For example: *Bridges.*

Following are some of the words which can be formed by using the letters *b r i d g e s*.

Bride	Bid	Gird	Ride
Bird	Big	Grid	Rig
Bred	Die	Red	Rise
Bed	Dig	Rib	Sir
Brig	Dire	Rid	Sire

No letter may be used oftener than it occurs in the selected word. There is *one E* in *bridge*. Therefore words like *breed, eider,* and *deer* cannot be formed from *bridge*. *S* cannot be used to form plurals. *Bride* and *brides, bird* and *birds,* are considered as the same word.

The educational value of this game is increased when simple definitions of every word must also be given, proving that the meaning of every word is understood. Of course, for younger children this need not be done.

A dictionary may be used for reference, but should not be consulted while the lists are being written.

An Educational Game

This game is a wonderful educator. It fixes the correct spelling of many words in mind and also increases the vocabulary.

Unknown words are frequently uncovered. For example, to the surprise of every one, *gride* and *erg* will be revealed as *real* words.

Some one may insist that *dyer* is spelled *dier*. The knowledge gained in this way is well learned.

Short words are better adapted for this game than long words containing too many vowels.

Lesson Six

There is scarcely any limit to the number of words which can be made from words like *elaborate* and *preparation,* but I prefer shorter words.

However, almost any word will furnish material for a good and resultful game.

The Game of Anagrams

The game of *Anagrams* is so well known that I will not take up space in describing it here. I recommend this game to young and old. It teaches spelling and develops quickness of mind.

Guessing Games

Many splendid guessing games increase our store of words, promote mental activity and develop the memory.

For example, there is the guessing game in which all the answers are the names of flowers.

Lists containing fifteen or twenty questions are given out, from which the following have been selected:

One end of the family pet.	Answer—*Cat-tail*
A nice man.	Answer—*Sweet William*
Things every one has.	Answer—*Tulips*
A part of the day.	Answer—*Four o'clock*

There are many other instructive games that are useful in spurring the mind to increased activity.

SUMMARY

1—The Mind's Eye in Spelling
2—Use of Exaggeration
3—Impressing the Troublesome Letter
4—Common-Sense Methods
5—Suggestions for Study
6—Initialing
7—Foreign Vocabularies
8—Aid for Postal Clerks
9—Developing Observation
10—Games that Improve the Memory

LESSON SEVEN

Practical Uses of the Roth Memory Course

This lesson contains a number of applications of the principles you have learned in the previous lessons. You will find all these examples worth your attention and helpful in business or social affairs.

Many students say these exercises have made them feel twenty years younger. All students who follow these lessons secure increased confidence and ability. They acquire a new interest and added power in their endeavors to reach the top.

The mental drill involved in learning and performing the Knight's Tour, the Card Feats, Mental Calendar Number Tests, and other applications is a great stimulant.

Three Things Are Necessary

1—*You must know your number code.*
2—*You must make proper associations.*
3—*You must review these associations until they become fixed in mind.*

I will give you a few instances of the use of the code.

Telephone Numbers

In Lesson Five you were shown how telephone numbers can be remembered by using the number code.

Here are a few illustrations showing how the name of the *exchange* can be associated with the number.

Names of Telephone Exchanges

In many cities the name of the *exchange* is suggested by the district in which the phone is located. Whenever necessary you can use *reminders* for the *exchanges*.

A Few Reminders for Exchanges

Cortland....**Court**	Rector......**Wreck**
Chelsea......**Shells**	Barclay.....**Bark**
Lenox.......**Lean Ox**	Harrison....**Hair**
Gramercy....**Grandma**	Schuyler....**Sky**
Main........**Mane**	Douglas.....**Glass**
Tabor.......**Taper**	West.......**Vest**
East........**Yeast**	Sutter......**Butter**
Beacon......**Lighthouse**	Bryant......**Brine**

Phone numbers and *exchanges* are linked with the *person* through *association*. This *association* can be either *visual* or association of thoughts without any pictures.

I shall give you a few examples of each.

Visual Method

Mr. **Baer.** Telephone number **Madison Square 4713.**

Madison Square suggests the reminder MAD. 4713 is represented by the code words *Rake, Team.* **Baer** naturally suggests *Bear.*

To form a picture combining these facts visualize:

A MAD *Bear* with a *Rake* chasing a *Team.*

In recalling this number, the name suggests *Bear.* This brings back the picture of:

The MAD *Bear*—MAD suggests *Madison Square.*

Rake and *Team* are the code words for 47—13.

Another Way

As you acquire fluency with the number code you will not have to depend upon your code words.

47 13 can be represented also by *Rocky Dam*.

Mr. *Baer*, telephone *Madison Square* **4713** can thus be converted into the following mental picture:

A MAD *Bear* on a *Rocky Dam*.

Association of Thought

The above telephone number can be kept in mind by the use of *association* of *thought*, instead of by mental picturing.

The following *thought* will serve our purpose nicely:

A *Bear* will be MAD if you throw a *Rock at Him*.

Note that *Rock at Him* represents **4713**.

Rock is 47, *at* is 1, *Him* is 3.

Consider these examples carefully, and better still, go over them a few times, using paper and pencil. Convert these associations into their corresponding numbers and the numbers into associations, without referring to the book. In this way you will acquire a ready ability to handle numbers of your own.

I can give you thousands of examples of the number code as used by myself and students in fixing telephone and other numbers in mind. I know it is better to cite a few illustrations that will be clear to you after careful consideration.

The important thing is for you to understand these examples and to apply the principles to those numbers of your own which you wish to keep in mind.

A Few Additional Examples

Roth Memory Institute Class Room. Tel. **Greeley 2582.**

25 82 is represented by *Only Fun.*

Greeley suggests the *reminder* REALLY.

The following thought holds this information in mind:
The *memory classes* are REALLY *only fun.* (No hard work involved.)

Majestic Hotel. Tel. Columbus 1900.

Fifth Avenue busses pass this hotel, so I formed the following association:

The busses CALL at the **Majestic.**

CALL is a *reminder* for **Columbus.**
The is 1, *busses* is 900, therefore *the busses* is **1900.**

A Coal Co. Tel. Capitol 3277.

The following served as a *reminder:*

The **Coal Co.'s** CAPITAL is in a *Mine* and the coal forms *coke.*
Mine is 32, *coke* is 77. *Mine coke* is **32 77.**

A Dock Co. Tel. Elliott 5031.

This information was retained by the following thought:

There is usually A LOT of *loose mud* about a **dock.**

Some minds may prefer to form a picture of **a dock** surrounded by *loose mud*—A LOT of it.

A LOT is a *reminder* for **Elliott.**
Loose is 50, *mud* is 31. *Loose mud* is **5031.**

Lesson Seven 247

Do not pass this illustration until you understand it thoroughly.

Harper and Bros. Tel. Beekman 3900.

I had occasion to call this number and the line was busy. I kept the number in mind readily by the following association:

They are BOOK MEN and *may possess* the facts I want.

BOOKMEN is a *reminder* for BEEKMAN.
May is 3, *possess* is 900. *May possess* is **3 900.**

Price Lists

To learn lot numbers and prices, convert them into words by means of the number code. These words must then be associated.

The following illustration will make this clear:

Lot No.	*Price*	*Association*	
301	$7.51	*Mist*	cloud
302	4.70	*Mason*	works
303	15.14	*Museum*	tall tree
304	5.10	*Miser*	holds
305	1.47	*Muscle*	drag
306	1.53	*Message*	tell me
307	6.26	*Mask*	change
308	5.71	*Home safe*	locked
309	13.95	*Mishap*	automobile
310	97.86	*Meets*	a big fish

Explanation:

The first lot number, **301,** is represented by the letters *m s t*. For these form the word *mist*.

The price of this item is **$7.51,** for which we have the sounds *k-l-d*. We combine these into the word *cloud*.

The association *Mist-cloud* converted into figures represents:

    Lot number **301,** *mist;* price **$7.51,** *cloud.*

In the same way *Mason-works* designates:

    Lot number **302,** *mason;* price **$4.70,** *works.*

The method will now be clear to you.

The next table illustrates how a student in the brass business made use of the number code.

He wished to keep in mind the following figures:

Weight Per 100 Square Inches of Sheet Brass

Gauge No.	*Weight*
8	3.9514
11	2.7903
14	1.9708
16	1.5625
18	1.2396
20	.9826

He converted the *Gauge* numbers, also the *Weight* figures, into words which were associated readily, as:

Gauge No		*Association*		*Weight*
8	Hive	*Maple*	*tree*	3.9514
11	Tied	*Neck*	*possum*	2.7903
14	Door	*To big*	*safe*	1.9708
16	Dish	*Tile*	*channel*	1.5625
18	Dove	*Hid in*	*ambush*	1.2396
20	News	*Boy*	*vanish*	9826

Gauge 8 was represented by *Hive*. This recalls the picture—*maple tree*—which was associated with *Hive*.

Lesson Seven

Maple tree represents 3 9 5 1 4.
Therefore Gauge 8 weighs **3.9514.**

Go over the remaining Gauge numbers and associations in the same manner and you will understand the method.

This student also wished to learn the following table:

Weight Per Foot of Round Brass Rod

Diameter in 1/8's	*Pounds per Foot*
1/8	.04527
2/8	.1811
3/8	.4074
4/8	.7243
7/8	2.218
9/8	3.667

He reversed the fractions **1/8, 2/8,** etc., writing them **81, 82, 83, 84, 87,** and **89,** and converted these into the corresponding code words.

These were associated with the words representing the pound per foot figures, as follows:

Diameter	*Association*		*Lbs. per Foot*
(81) Foot	Sore	lynx	.045270
(82) Fan	Devoted		.1811
(83) Foam	Race	car	.4074
(84) Fire	Gun	ram	.7243
(87) Fig	No	native	2.218
(89) Fop	Much	joke	3.667

To recall the weight for any given diameter, as for example 1/8 inch, reverse 1/8, giving the figures **81.**

The code word for **81** is *Foot.*

Foot suggests the associated picture—*sore-lynx.*

Sore-lynx—*s-r-l-n-k-s*—converted into numbers gives us 045270.

The explanation of these methods takes more time than the actual process.

Use this plan for

> *Price Lists.*
> *Catalog Figures.*
> *Insurance Rates.*
> *Statistics of all kinds.*

This method will be easy after you know your code.

Stop Payment Checks

Bank tellers often find it a serious problem to remember the checks on which payment has been stopped.

There are several ways in which this difficulty can be overcome, depending on local conditions.

In many large banks it is customary to cash no check dated more than two days back. In this way the teller has to keep in mind the stop-payments of two days only. If a check of earlier date is presented, the paying teller refers to records showing older stop payments.

Use Visualization

The various principles of visualization and association can be applied to remember current stop-payment checks. The means employed by each teller depends largely on the kind of memory he has.

A teller with a strong visual memory is able to see in his *mind's eye* the checks on which payment has been stopped. He visualizes the amount and the signature, which is usually a familiar one.

Another good method which may be used when the individual who drew the check is familiar, is to visualize

Lesson Seven 251

the person's appearance. This serves as a reminder that he has ordered a check stopped.

Make Words for Amounts

One of the best methods for the student who knows the number code, is to make words for the amounts of the various checks on which payment has been stopped, and to associate these words with one another or with the issuer.

This is of special value in places where many pay checks are issued by one or two large companies. In such cases many checks may have the same signature.

A mental picture can be formed representing the issuer of the check and the object designating the amount. The following example will explain in detail.

A teller in a bank which did a large business with a mining company had considerable trouble with the checks which were lost each month by careless miners.

Finally he pictured the engine shed of the mine, and put the objects representing the amounts of the checks on the roof, in the doorway, attached to the flywheel of the engine, etc.

The first check on which payment was stopped was for $86.15. He pictured a large *fish-tail* hanging from the chimney.

Fish tail represents 86.15.

He was next told to stop payment on a check for $107.00, and he pictured the engineer sitting on a bright new desk.

Desk designates 107.

He had six other checks on which payment was stopped, and for these he formed picture associations in the same manner. This solved the problem for him in a most satisfactory way.

A Convenient Method

Some students find it convenient to use long words and consider only the first three sounds in the words, when transposed into figures.

For example:

Relative	to represent	451
Rascals	" "	407
Navigate	" "	287
Pavement	" "	983

You may find it desirable to adopt this method. Let me caution you that you can use it successfully only if you follow it strictly. If you use pavement to represent 983, never use it to represent 9832 or 98321.

The Calendar Feat

To Calculate the Day for Any Date Instantly

Most of us are limited in the use of the calendar to the year in which we are living. We cannot go behind the first of last January or beyond the thirty-first of next December without considerable figuring.

The calendar seems a difficult piece of mechanism. We must even depend upon a bit of doggerel to remind us of those months which have thirty-one days and those which have only thirty.

As Simple as Addition

But the calendar is really as *simple* as a sum in addition. It is also a wonderful convenience and can be made to furnish a lot of fun. It is as easy to know what day

Lesson Seven

January 1, 2016, will fall upon as to learn what day the first of the coming month will be. *It is a mere matter of addition and division.*

Keep a calendar before you as I explain the basis and you will follow me readily.

It is the *odd* day of *each year* and the *odd* days of the *month* which make the calendar computation appear difficult. But when you go at it systematically you will see that it is quite easy.

Month Values and Year Values

Our calculations are based upon certain *month values* and certain *year values*.

The *month values* represent the sum of the odd days left over from the previous months. **January**, being the first month, has no odd days to inherit from the previous month, so its *month value* is **0**.

January itself has 3 odd days and an even number of weeks. It is the *three odd days* which make the difference in day between any date in January and the same date in February.

Therefore **February** has the value of **3**.

If you will look at your calendar you will see that *any date in February falls three days later in the week than the same date in January*.

Use of the Calendar

Look again at your calendar and you will note—unless it be leap year—the dates in **March** fall upon the *same* days of the week as in **February**. This is because **February** has four even weeks. *No odd days accumulate in February*.

March also has the value of **3**.

March again has 3 odd days, which, added to the **3** odd days previously considered, gives a total of **6** which has accumulated up to April.

April therefore has the value of **6**.

April, in turn, has 2 odd days which, added to the **6** already accumulated, gives us **8** odd days.

Since 7 days equal a full week and have no effect upon the results we seek, we subtract 7, which leaves **1** as the value of **May**.

Seven Subtracted Does Not Change Result

Look at your calendar and you will see that **1** and **8**—the 1st and the 8th—always fall upon the same day.

May has 3 odd days, which, added to the **1** odd day brought over from April, gives us a value of **4** for **June**.

June has 2 odd days, which, added to the 4 brought over, gives us a value of **6** for **July**.

July has 3 odd days, which, added to the **6**, gives us **9**. We here again drop 7 and have remaining as the value of **August, 2**.

August has 3 odd days, which, added to the **2**, gives us a value of **5** for **September**.

September has 2 odd days, which, added to the **5**, gives us **7**. This we drop and give **October** a value of **0**.

Look at your calendar and you will see that 7, added to or taken from any date, does not change the day of the week.

October has 3 odd days. This gives **November** a value of **3**.

November has 2 odd days, which, added to the **3**, gives us **5** as the **December** value.

I have taken you through these figures to indicate the method. *You will not have to go through this process every time.* The results are found in the following table.

Table of Month Values

In the table which follows, the first letter of each monthly code word indicates the initial letter of the month. The last consonant of each code word indicates the value of the month, as for instance:

The code word for January is **Joys**. J stands for *January* and S for **0**.

Month	Value	Code	Month	Value	Code
January	0	**Joys**	July	6	**Judge**
February	3	**Foam**	August	2	**Ann**
March	3	**Mummy**	September	5	**Seal**
April	6	**Ash**	October	0	**Oh! See**
May	1	**Mate**	November	3	**Nome**
June	4	**Junior**	December	5	**Doll**

These month values never change—they are the same every year.

Year Value

Every normal year has 52 weeks, plus *one* day.

In other words, every year is made up of 52 full weeks and one extra day, except leap year, which has two extra days.

This accounts for the fact that if January 1st of this year falls upon Monday, next year it will fall upon Tuesday, unless this year is leap year. In that case January of next year would fall upon Wednesday.

Since each year has either 1 or 2 odd days, in figuring succeeding years the only changes are the figure 1, for normal years, and the figure 2, for leap years.

Twentieth Century Table

Beginning with 1900, which has a year value of **0**, you will find in the following table of 100 years an increase of 1 or 2 in the figure value of each year.

Observe that no year has a greater figure value than 6. We always consider **7** as having the value of **0**. You have already seen that 7 added to, or taken away from, any date does not make any change in the week day.

Year	Year Figure	Reminder	Year	Year Figure	Reminder
1900	0	*Icy* Sauce	1924	2	*New* Snare
1901	1	*Odd* Hat	1925	3	*Home* Nail
1902	2	*New* Hen	1926	4	*Wire* Hinge
1903	3	*My* Ham	1927	5	*Yellow* Ink
1904	5	*Yellow* Hare	**1928**	0	*Saw* Knife
1905	6	*Showy* Hill	1929	1	*White* Knob
1906	0	*Sew* Shoe	1930	2	*New* Moose
1907	1	*White* Cow	1931	3	*My* Mud
1908	3	*My* Hive	**1932**	5	*Yellow* Moon
1909	4	*Hairy* Ape	1933	6	*Show* Mummy
1910	5	*Low* Woods	1934	0	*Use* Hammer
1911	6	*Wash* Tide	1935	1	*White* Mule
1912	1	*Heat* Tin	**1936**	3	*Home* Match
1913	2	*New* Team	1937	4	*Weary* Hammock
1914	3	*My* Tire	1938	5	*Yellow* Muff
1915	4	*Weary* Hotel	1939	6	*Huge* Mop
1916	6	*Showy* Dish	**1940**	1	*White* Rose
1917	0	*Wise* Dog	1941	2	*Annoy* Rat
1918	1	*White* Dove	1942	3	*Home* Rain
1919	2	*New* Tub	1943	4	*Hairy* Ram
1920	4	*Wire* Nose	**1944**	6	*Huge* Warrior
1921	5	*Holy* Window	1945	0	*Icy* Rail
1922	6	*Shy* Nun	1946	1	*White* Roach
1923	0	*Wise* Gnome	1947	2	*New* Rake

LESSON SEVEN 257

Year	Year Figure	Reminder	Year	Year Figure	Reminder
1948	4	*Airy* Roof	1974	1	*White* Car
1949	5	*Oily* Rope	1975	2	*No* Coal
1950	6	*Showy* Lace	**1976**	4	*Wire* Cage
1951	0	*See* Light	1977	5	*Yellow* Cake
1952	2	*Wan* Lion	1978	6	*Wash* Cuff
1953	3	*Home* Lime	1979	0	*Whose* Cab
1954	4	*Weary* Lawyer	**1980**	2	*New* Vase
1955	5	*Yellow* Lily	1981	3	*My* Foot
1956	0	*Wise* Lodge	1982	4	*Air* Fan
1957	1	*Wide* Lake	1983	5	*Yellow* Foam
1958	2	*New* Loaf	**1984**	0	*House* Fire
1959	3	*My* Lap	1985	1	*Hot* File
1960	5	*Yellow* Cheese	1986	2	*Any* Fish
1961	6	*Huge* Sheet	1987	3	*My* Fig
1962	0	*Icy* Chain	**1988**	5	*Yellow* Fife
1963	1	*Hot* Jam	1989	6	*Showy* Fob
1964	3	*Home* Chair	1990	0	*Use* Bus
1965	4	*Wire* Jail	1991	1	*Wet* Boat
1966	5	*Oily* Judge	**1992**	3	*Home* Piano
1967	6	*Huge* Check	1993	4	*Air* Bomb
1968	1	*Haughty* Chief	1994	5	*Yellow* Bear
1969	2	*New* Ship	1995	6	*Hush* Bell
1970	3	*Aim* Goose	**1996**	1	*Odd* Bush
1971	4	*Air* Kite	1997	2	*In* Bag
1972	6	*Ash* Can	1998	3	*Home* Beef
1973	0	*Whose* Comb	1999	4	*Air* Pipe

Note: The leap years are indicated by heavy type.

The *code* word represents the *year;* the first word gives the *figure* value of that year.

For example, *Sew Shoe:*

The code word *Shoe* represents the year 6, in other words, **1906.**

Sew gives you the figure value of this year—1906—which is **0**.

Therefore *Sew Shoe*, converted into figures, means:

Figure value **0**—*year* **1906**.

Rule

To find the day of the week for any date, add together the year figure, the month figure, and the date. Divide by seven. The remainder gives the day of the week, as explained below.

A few examples will make the working of this rule clear. It is exceedingly simple.

To find the day of the week for *December* 25, 1981:

    Year figure—1981   *My*   3
    Month   "   Dec.   *Doll* 5
    Date   25
                                                 ——
                                               33

Divide 33 by 7. The remainder—5—represents *Friday*, the fifth day after Sunday as per the following table:

Day Value of Remainder

When dividing the total by 7, if there is no remainder, the day is **Sunday**. The other days are indicated by remainders as follows:

    1......Monday   **4**......Thursday
    2......Tuesday   **5**......Friday
    3......Wednesday **6**......Saturday

LESSON SEVEN 259

You have no idea how easy it is to figure the day of the week until you try it a few times.

Begin with dates in the years 1917, 1918, and 1919.

All you need to carry in mind are the figure value of the months and the year value of these three years, which are as follows:

    1917—*wise* dog 0
    1918—*white* dove 1
    1919—*new* tub 2

See how easily you can figure these dates:

January 15, 1918

Merely add together:

    1 for 1918
    0 for January
    15 for the date

This gives a total of 16.

Divide by 7, leaving a remainder of 2—*Tuesday*.

February 15, 1918

Add together:

    1 for 1918
    3 for February
    15 for the date

Total is 19, which, divided by 7, leaves a remainder of 5—*Friday*.

April 16, 1919

Add together:

    2 for 1919
    6 for April
    16 for the date

The sum is 24, which, divided by 7, leaves a remainder of 3—*Wednesday.*

Value for Other Centuries

The year figures given for the years 1900 to 1999 can also be used in other centuries by the addition of a century figure as follows:

        18th Century (1700's)—4
        19th   "   (1800's)—2
        21st   "   (2000's)—6

Examples:

August 12, 1755

    Century figure............. 4
    Year figure —*yellow*....... 5
    Month figure—*Ann*........ 2
    Date..................... 12
                             —
                            23

Divide 23 by 7 and you have a remainder of 2. The day is *Tuesday.*

October 22, 1865

    Century figure............. 2
    Year figure —*wire*......... 4
    Month figure—*oh! see*....... 0
    Date..................... 22
                             —
                            28

Divide 28 by 7. There is no remainder, hence the day is *Sunday*.

June 20, 2018
    Century figure............. 6
    Year figure —*white*........ 1
    Month figure—*junior*....... 4
    Date..................... 20
                            ——
                            31

Divide 31 by 7 and you have a remainder of 3—*Wednesday*.

Note that in the 18th century—the 1700's, our computations go back only to 1753. This is because there was a change in the calendar in 1752.

You will find an interesting history of the calendar in the Encyclopedia Britannica. This is well worth reading.

One more point and then you will have the complete method. You must understand the leap-year rule.

Leap-Year Rule

In figuring dates in January or February of leap years always deduct 1.

Examples:

January 11, 1920
    Century figure............. 0
    Year   —*wire*............. 4
    January—*joys*............. 0
    Date..................... 11
                            ——
                            15
    Deduct................... 1
                            ——
                            14

Divide 14 by 7. There is no remainder, hence the day is *Sunday*.

February 29, 1844

Century figure.............	2
Year —*huge*..............	6
Month—*foam*.............	3
Date.....................	29
	40
Deduct..................	1
	39

Divide 39 by 7. There is a remainder of 4, which signifies *Thursday*.

January 15, 2000

Century figure.............	6
Year —*icy*...............	0
Month—*joys*..............	0
Date.....................	15
	21
Deduct..................	1
	20

Divide 20 by 7. There is a remainder of 6—*Saturday*.

The year 2000 will be a leap year. 1700, 1800, and 1900 were not leap years.

Mental Calculation

With a little practice you can figure any date mentally. This is excellent exercise in many ways. See if you can get the correct answers for the following *leap year* dates *Be sure and deduct* 1 *in each instance.*

February 19, 1896	Answer, *Wednesday*
January 25, 1924	Answer, *Friday*
February 29, 2000	Answer, *Tuesday*
January 15, 1784	Answer, *Thursday*

Caution. The deduction of 1 is made only in January and February of leap years. Do not make the mistake of deducting 1 in any other months.

Additional Examples for Practice

See if you can get the correct solution to each of these.

Answer	*Answer*
Sept. 16, 1805—*Mon.*	Feb. 19, 1916—*Sat.*
Oct. 24, 1765—*Thurs.*	Aug. 39, 1921—*Tues.*
Jan. 18, 1920—*Sun.*	Mar. 9, 1900—*Fri.*
Dec. 16, 1905—*Sat.*	June 22, 1916—*Thurs.*
April 19, 1777—*Sat.*	July 4, 1899—*Tues.*
May 6, 1868—*Wed.*	Nov. 19, 1917—*Mon.*
Jan. 1, 1919—*Wed.*	April 12, 1918—*Fri.*
July 4, 1918—*Thurs.*	Feb. 17, 1919—*Mon.*
Nov. 2, 1920—*Tues.*	June 15, 2018—*Fri.*
Dec. 25, 1918—*Wed.*	July 4, 1918—*Thurs.*

A Wonderful Card Feat

If interested in card playing, the code enables you to perform an interesting and amazing feat. This was devised and first used by my friend, Henry Hatton.

You will be able to remember the order of every card in a deck.

This is a memory performance and not a card trick. Your code words enable you to keep in mind the location of every card as it is called.

It is necessary to represent every one of the fifty-two

cards in the deck by a special word. These words you can form yourself.

The cards in every suit are numbered from **1** to **13**, the *Ace* being **1**, and the *King* being considered as **13**.

Let S be our symbol for *Spades*. *S* will be the first letter in thirteen code words representing the thirteen *Spade cards*. The last sound in each of these words will represent the number of the card, this last sound being based upon the number code.

Spade Symbols

Thus the *ace of Spades* will be represented by any word beginning with *S* to designate *Spades* and ending with *T* or *D* representing *one*. The words *Sot, Soot, Suit, Sod, Sud* will designate the *ace of Spades*. We will use the word *Suit*.

Any of the words *Son, Sun, Sign, Seine* will properly stand for the *deuce of Spades*,—*S* for *Spades* and *N* for **2**. We select *Sun*.

The words *Seam, Siam, Sam, Swim* will mean the *three of Spades*. We choose *Seam*.

The words *Sore, Sewer, Seer, Sour, Sire* will represent the *four of Spades*. We will take *Sewer*.

Symbols for Other Cards

In the same way words can be formed to designate the *Club* cards, every word beginning with *C* to stand for *Clubs,* and containing the letters to represent the *number* of the card.

A similar list is made for the *Heart* cards beginning with *H*, designating *Hearts,* and for the *Diamond* cards beginning with *D*, for *Diamonds*.

The following list contains a name for all the cards in the deck. As you have seen, there are many other words which can be used. If you prefer you can prepare your own list.

Card Words

Cards	Spades	Hearts	Clubs	Diamonds
Ace	Suit	Hut	Cat	Dude
2	Sun	Hone	Cane	Den
3	Seam	Home	Comb	Dam
4	Sewer	Hair	Car	Door
5	Seal	Hail	Coal	Doll
6	Sash	Hash	Cash	Dodge
7	Sock	Hook	Cook	Duck
8	Safe	Hoof	Cuff	Dive
9	Soap	Hoop	Cape	Dupe
10	Suds	Heads	Cots	Dates
J	Statue	Hooded	Cadet	Dotted
Q	Stone	Heathen	Cotton	Dayton
K	Steam	Hay time	Coy dame	Diadem

When you are familiar with these words it is an easy matter to memorize the position of each card in a deck as they are called off to you.

For actual entertainment purposes it is better to use only thirty-two cards, as it takes less time, making the feat all the more interesting. For practice use the entire pack.

The Method

For example, let us say the *first* card in the pack is the *five of Clubs*, which is represented by the word *Coal*. Your first code word is *Hat* and you merely make a picture of a *Hat* full of *Coal*.

The *second* card may be the *ace of Hearts*, which is represented by the word *Hut*. Combine this in a picture with your second code word, *Hen*.

The *third* card may be the *six of Clubs*, which is designated by *Cash*. Make a picture of *Ham* and *Cash*.

The *fourth* card by way of illustration is the *seven of Spades*. See the *Hare* and *Sock* together.

The *fifth* card is the *Jack of Spades*. Associate *Hill* with *Statue*.

Associate Code and Card Words

In the same way picture each *card word* in order with the corresponding *code word*.

Be careful not to disarrange the order of the cards. After you have formed all your associations hand the pack to some one else to verify them as you name them.

To call the *first card* you refer to your first code word, which is *Hat*. This will recall your picture of *Hat* and *Coal*, which represents the *five* of *Clubs*.

Hen will suggest your *second* card word, the *Hut*, which stands for the *ace of Hearts*.

The *third* card will be recalled by the *Ham* and the *Cash*. This designates the *six of Clubs* as your *third* card.

Card number *four* is revived by the picture of the *Hare* and the *Sock*, giving us *seven of Spades*.

The *fifth* card is remembered by the *Statue* on the *Hill*. *Statue* is the *Jack of Spades*, so card number *five* is the *Jack of Spades*.

Code Will Recall Card Words

In the same way every code word will recall the card word with which it has been pictured.

Practice by yourself before you attempt to perform this before a group of friends or an audience. You must

LESSON SEVEN   267

know your card words. This can be done only through
regular practice.

*You must be sure to form a picture of every card word
and the corresponding code word.*

I recommend the mastery of this feat to all my students,
as it is both entertaining and stimulating. No one can
get too much exercise in visualization and the practice
will be a general mental tonic.

The Tour of the Knight

This is a splendid and interesting memory test and
does not require any previous knowledge of chess.

The problem is to call from memory every move of the
Chess Knight, beginning with any square which may be
selected. Note the accompanying diagram and see that
the squares are numbered from 1 to 64.

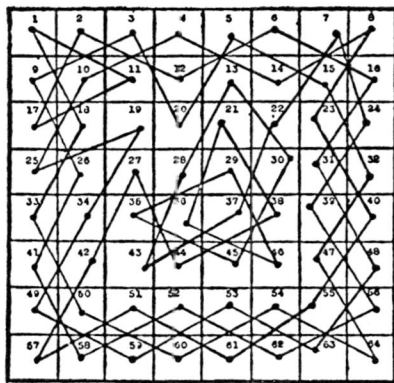

The illustration shows the moves of the Knight beginning with square 1. The Knight has a peculiar move,

going two squares in one direction and one in the other, as shown by the line drawn from 1 to 11, 11 to 17, and so on.

Observe that the Knight stops at every one of the 64 squares, once only.

This feat can be performed in public by using a large blackboard or sheet of cardboard on which are drawn the 64 squares representing the 64 squares of the chessboard. These are numbered from 1 to 64.

You stand with your back to the blackboard. As you call every move of the Knight a line is drawn by some one else connecting the square just left and the new square occupied.

Any student of these lessons who wishes to perform this spectacular feat and call the sixty-four moves in their proper order from memory can do so if he has learned his number code.

The Moves of the Knight

Observe your diagram and see that the moves are as follows:

1	48	10	51	46	37	58	32
11	63	4	57	29	22	41	47
17	53	14	42	35	7	26	64
2	59	8	27	45	24	9	54
12	49	23	44	30	39	3	60
6	34	40	38	13	56	20	50
16	19	55	21	28	62	5	33
31	25	61	36	43	52	15	18

These moves are kept in mind by learning the following words, which as you will see, represent these numbers in their correct order.

LESSON SEVEN 269

In learning this series of words combine *visualization* and *logical association*. The first three words—*toe, toad,* and *toga*—have a similar sound and this will aid you. Note also the likeness of sound in *jam-lamb, leap-reap, weary-dreary,* and *mule-rule.*

Easily Learned

Go through the list and see how easily it is learned. Use any principle that will assist you. Also associate the last word, *tough,* with the first word, *toe.* Then you will have an endless chain. This is necessary to perform the Knight's Tour, as you must always return to the starting point.

1—Toe	10—Doze	46—Rich	58—Laugh
11—Toad	4—Weary	29—Unhappy	41—Rude
17—Toga	14—Dreary	35—Mule	26—Enjoy
2—New	8—Waif	45—Rule	9—Happy
12—Town	23—Enemy	30—Messiah	3—Home
6—Show	40—Rouse	13—Tomb	20—Nice
16—Teach	55—Hallelujah	28—Enough	5—Holy
31—Mad	61—Shout	43—Room	15—Toil
48—Rough	51—Lad	37—Hammock	32—Money
63—Jam	57—Lake	22—Noon	47—Work
53—Lamb	42—Rain	7—Gay	64—Cheer
59—Leap	27—Ink	24—Nero	54—Holler
49—Reap	44—Horror	39—Imp	60—Chase
34—More	38—Movie	56—Hellish	50—Lazy
19—Dope	21—Annoyed	62—Shine	33—Mummy
25—Inhale	36—Homage	52—Lion	18—Tough

When you know the words and are able to convert them quickly into their respective numbers you may allow any one to choose any square on the board as a starting place. It is not necessary to begin with number 1.

For example, if 44 is selected as the square from which the Knight is to start, in your series the word *horror* represents 44, so you begin with *horror* and call up the next word, which is *movie*. This gives you 38 as the next move. In this way proceed through the list until you reach the last word, *tough,* 18. To complete the circle you must go from *tough* to *toe,* 1, and continue until you again reach the word *horror*. This completes the tour and returns the Knight to the starting point.

So you see it does not matter where the Knight starts. The procedure is always the same, as you go from the starting square to 18, then to 1 and continue until you again reach the original square selected.

Good Exercise

The Knight's Tour is interesting and affords good practice on the code, as well as being stimulating, wholesome mental exercise. By all means learn it and perform it frequently.

You will understand readily that the number code can be applied to memorizing figures and statistics of any kind.

The figures must be converted into a word or words and associated with the fact itself. I could give you many illustrations but they would not prove of as much value as working out your own cases.

History Dates

In former years students of history were forced to learn many dates. Modern instructors do not require this, and wisely so.

LESSON SEVEN

However, the number code enables the student who has need for such figures to remember them readily. The following illustrations show the use of the code for remembering dates.

The European War began:
July 28, 1914

July is the *seventh* month, so July 28, 1914, is represented by 7-28-14.

We need not bother about the figure 19 as we know the date was 1914, not 1814.

We now convert the figures 7-28-14 into words.

For 728 we have *gun off*.

For 14 we use *dire*.

We fix this in mind with a sentence, as:

The **Great War** was caused by an assassin who shot a *gun off* with *dire* results. The exact phraseology is not important. The things to associate in the mind are:

War—*Gun off*—*Dire*

Another noteworthy fact:

The opening of the Panama Canal:
August 15, 1914—8-15-14

The gate of the **Panama Canal** is a *heavy toll door*.
Heavy, 8 *Toll,* 15 *Door,* 14

Russia stopped the sale of intoxicants:
August 20, 1914—8-20-14

Fancy **Russia** doing such a thing. *Water* will be their beverage.

Fancy, 820 *Water,* 14

The Baltimore fire:

February 7, 1904—2-7-04

The **Baltimore** fire burned fiercely—*no geyser* could extinguish it.

No is 2   *Geyser*, 7-04

The North Pole was discovered by Peary:

April 6, 1909—4-6-09

Peary *reaches up* and plants the United States flag at the *N o r t h   P o l e* .

Reaches, 460   *Up*, 9

The Union Pacific Railroad was opened:

May 10, 1869—5-10-69

The building of the **Union Pacific** through the *wilds* was a *job*.

Wilds, 510   *Job*, 69

The Battle of Waterloo:

June 18, 1815—6-18-815

At **Waterloo** cannon were *shot off* with *fatal* results.

Shot off, 618   *Fatal*, 815

President Lincoln's assassination:

April 14, 1865—4-14-65

Our dear **Lincoln** was killed by a *shallow* knave.

Our, 4   *Dear*, 14   *Shallow*, 65

Lesson Seven

Boston Tea Party:

December 16, 1773—12-16-73

They threw the **Tea** *down* in the *ditch* as they *came*.

Down, 12 *Ditch*, 16 *Came*, 73

Postal Banks established in the United States:

January 3, 1911—1-3-11

The establishing of the **Postal Banks** was no *tame deed*.

Tame, 13 *Deed*, 11

The San Francisco fire:

April 18, 1906—4-18-06

The **San Francisco** fire covered a wide *area*, and was a *tough siege* for the inhabitants.

Area, 4 *Tough*, 18 *Siege*, 06

By following this method systematically, forming good associations and reviewing them regularly, any dates or statistics may be fixed in mind.

Chemistry

Atomic weights are easy for some students but prove difficult to others. If you need help use means like the following:

Aluminum—atomic weight 27.

Aluminum is essentially a *Yankee* metal.

If you prefer to use a *mind's eye* picture you can visualize an *aluminum* cup filled with *ink*.

Yankee and *ink* both represent 27.

Should you be interested in chemistry you will find it good practice to go through the table of elements and learn the atomic weights in this way.

Aid for Bible Students

The various principles for strengthening the memory can be applied in many ways to Bible study.

The location of any verse can be fixed in mind by some such association as illustrated in the following examples:

The story of the *Prodigal Son* is found in the 15th chapter of Luke. This can be fixed in mind by the thought,

The father Looked Daily for the Prodigal Son.

Looked suggests Luke, and *Daily* represents 15—in other words, Luke XV.

The location of the *Ten Commandments,* Exodus XX, is recalled by the thought that they represent *Excellent News.*

Excellent suggests *Exodus,* and *News* stands for 20.

The verse *"Ask and it shall be given you"* is found in Matthew VII, 7.

The sentence *Ask Matthew to have some cake* conveys this information.

Cake represents VII, 7

The student interested in this subject can make many applications of this form of association. If these phrases are reviewed a few times they will become fixed in mind. Going over them once is not sufficient.

The Books of the Bible

Many of my students have enjoyed learning the order of the Books of the Bible, and the number of Chapters in each book. This is done easily and is good practice in the number code also in mental picturing and association.

The Books, their order and the number of chapters in each, can be learned quickly by making use of the code and association. The *reminder* for each Book and the word representing the number of chapters are linked with the proper code word.

Books and Chapters of Old Testament

The following table will be understood readily by every student who has followed the principles outlined in the previous lessons:

No.	Book	Chp.	Code	Rem'der	Chp.
1	Genesis	50	HAT	*Gentle*	Lass
2	Exodus	40	HEN	*Exit*	Race
3	Levit.	27	HAM	*Leave*	Now go
4	Numbers	36	HARE	*Number*	Much
5	Deuter.	34	HILL	*Dew*	More
6	Joshua	24	SHOE	*Josh*	Narrow
7	Judges	21	COW	*Judges*	Ant
8	Ruth	4	HIVE	*Root*	Hair
9	I Sam'l	31	APE	*Some*	Meat
10	II Sam'l	24	WOODS	*Same*	Winner
11	I Kings	22	TIDE	*King*	Union
12	II Kings	25	TIN	*Kings*	Only
13	I Chron.	29	TEAM	*Crown*	Nobby
14	II Chron.	36	TIRE	*Cronies*	Image
15	Ezra	10	HOTEL	*Ezra*	Dizzy
16	Nehem.	13	DISH	*Near my*	Thumb
17	Esther	10	DOG	*Pester*	Tease

No.	Book	Chp.	Code	Rem'der	Chp.
18	Job	42	DOVE	*Job*	Run
19	Psalms	150	TUB	*Palm*	Towels
20	Prov'rbs	31	NOSE	*Prove*	Might
21	Eccles.	12	WINDOW	*Ache*	Done
22	Song Sol.	8	NUN	*Song*	Vow
23	Isaiah	66	GNOME	*Icy*	Judge
24	Jerem.	52	SNARE	*Jeer*	Lion
25	Lament.	5	NAIL	*Lame*	Heel
26	Ezekiel	48	HINGE	*Squeak*	Rough
27	Daniel	12	INK	*Daniel*	Den
28	Hosea	14	KNIFE	*Hose*	Tear
29	Joel	3	KNOB	*Jewel*	Hem
30	Amos	9	MOOSE	*Aim*	Boy
31	Obadiah	1	MUD	*A bad*	Toy
32	Jonah	4	MOON	*Join*	Wire
33	Micah	7	MUMMY	*Mike*	Wake
34	Nahum	3	HAMMER	*Name*	Aim
35	Habak.	3	MULE	*Cook*	Home
36	Zephan.	3	MATCH	*Zephyr*	Hum
37	Haggai	2	HAMMOCK	*Hag*	In
38	Zechar.	14	MUFF	*Sack*	Tear
39	Malachi	4	MOP	*Mallet*	Hero

Books and Chapters of New Testament

No.	Book	Chp.	Code	Rem'der	Chp.
1	Matthew	28	HAT	*Mat*	Navy
2	Mark	16	HEN	*Mark*	Ditch
3	Luke	24	HAM	*Lucky*	Winner
4	John	21	HARE	*Join*	Net
5	Acts	28	HILL	*Axe*	Knife
6	Romans	16	SHOE	*Romans*	Dutch
7	1st Cor.	16	COW	*Corn*	Dish
8	2nd Cor.	13	HIVE	*Corn*	Tomb
9	Galat.	6	APE	*Gay*	Joy

Lesson Seven

No.	Book	Chp.	Code	Rem'der	Chp.
10	Ephes.	6	WOODS	*Fashion*	Show
11	Phillip	4	TIDE	*Fill*	Hurry
12	Coloss.	4	TIN	*Call*	War
13	1st Thess.	5	TEAM	*Thistle*	Haul
14	2nd Thess.	3	TIRE	*Thistle*	Home
15	1st. Tim.	6	HOTEL	*Time*	Chew
16	2nd Tim.	4	DISH	*Timothy*	Raw
17	Titus	3	DOG	*Tied*	Ham
18	Philem.	1	DOVE	*Film*	White
19	Hebrews	13	TUB	*Brews*	Steam
20	James	5	NOSE	*Games*	Howl
21	1st Peter	5	WINDOW	*Beat her*	Yell
22	2nd Peter	3	NUN	*Repeat*	Hymn
23	1st John	5	GNOME	*John*	Hello
24	2nd John	1	SNARE	*Johnny*	Ahead
25	3rd John	1	NAIL	*Join*	Hut
26	Jude	1	HINGE	*Dude*	Tea
27	Revel.	22	INK	*Rebel*	Union

You can revise these tables to suit your own memory. This will be good practice and the lists and associations which you originate will be more readily retained.

With a little care there will be no confusion in using the same list of code words for both the Old and the New Testament.

Memory Rhymes

Rhymes Aid the Memory

A few years ago the following striking illustration of the shortcomings of the average memory appeared in the daily papers:

WRITE A POEM AND REMEMBER YOUR AGE

United States Health Bureau Suggests Jingles Such as "In 1882 Little Susie Began to Boo"

Washington, March 13.—The inability of the average person to remember his age and the year of his birth, together with the suggestion that a person's birth year be made the subject of a rhyme as an aid to memory is the subject of a bulletin issued by the United States public health service. It is a common occurrence to find school children, even high-school pupils, who cannot tell how old they are, or who, if they know their age, cannot tell accurately in what year they were born, says the bulletin. It adds that this information will be necessary in securing a marriage license or in registering for voting; in seeking a government position or in claiming a fortune.

As an aid to the remembrance of a person's age and his birth year the formation of a rhyme or jingle is recommended by the bulletin. "In 1897 little Johnnie came from heaven," or "In 1882 little Susie began to boo," are two samples of the poetic efforts of the officials who apologize for their efforts, however, by saying *"Never mind what the rhyme is, just so you remember it."*

Use This Principle if It Helps

You have doubtless learned from experience the value of rhymes in fixing facts in mind. Almost every one depends on the following bit of doggerel to remember the number of days in the month:

> Thirty days hath September,
> April, June and November.

Southey, the poet, wrote the following as a memory aid for his daughter:

> A cow's daughter is called a *calf;*
> A sheep's child a *lamb.*
> My darling must not say *"I are,"*
> But always say *"I am."*

Here are a few examples which may prove of value to adults and to children. They have been of help to many teachers in driving these facts home.

Nine Parts of Speech

Three little words you often see
Are articles *a, an* and *the.*
A noun's the name of anything,
As *school* or *garden, hoop* or *swing.*
Adjectives tell the kind of noun,
As *great, small, pretty, white* or *brown.*

Instead of nouns the pronouns stand—
Her head, *his* face, *your* arm, *my* hand.
Verbs tell of something to be done—
To *read, count, sing, laugh, jump* or *run.*
How things are done, the adverbs tell,
As *slowly, quickly, ill* or *well.*
Conjunctions couple words together,
As clear *and* cold *but* pleasant weather.

The preposition stands before
A noun, as *in,* or *through* a door.
The interjection shows surprise,
As *Oh!* how pretty, *Ah!* how wise.
The whole are called Nine Parts of Speech,
Which reading, writing, speaking teach.

How to Learn the Piano Keys

All the G and A keys
Are between the black *threes;*
And 'tween the *twos* are all the D's;
Then on the *right* side of the threes
Will be found the B's and C's;
But on the *left* side of the threes
Are all the F's and all the E's.

Sharps and Flats

A-MAJOR key *three sharps* will tell;
The MINOR-*A* is *natural;*
And *A-flat*-MAJOR all will say,
With *four flats* ever we must play.

Sharps and Flats—*Continued*

With MAJOR-*B five sharps* are sent;
B-MINOR is with *two* content;
To *B-flat*-MAJOR *two flats* place;
With *B-flat*-MINOR *five flats* trace.

To prove our maxim plain and true,
C-MAJOR key we *natural* view.
On MINOR-*C three flats* attend;
And *C-sharp*-MINOR *four* befriend.

The MAJOR-*D two sharps* doth crave;
The MINOR-*D one flat* must have;
With *D-flat*-MAJOR *five* are told;
With *D-sharp*-MINOR *six* behold.

With MAJOR-*E four sharps* we'll own;
The MINOR-*E* has only *one;*
To *E-flat*-MAJOR *three flats* fix,
As *E-flat*-MINOR must have *six.*

F-MAJOR key has *one* poor *flat;*
The MINOR-*F* has *four* times that;
For *F-sharp*-MAJOR *six sharps* score;
To *F-sharp*-MINOR three—no more.

G-MAJOR key with *one sharp* make;
G-MINOR key *two flats* will take;
To *G-sharp*-MAJOR *five sharps* name;
And *G-flat*-MINOR *six flats* claim.

The Books of the Old Testament

In *Genesis*, the world was made,
  By God's Almighty hand;
In *Exodus*, the Hebrews marched
  To gain the promised land.
Leviticus contains the law,
  Holy and just and good;
Numbers records the tribes enrolled—
  All sons of Abraham's blood.
Moses in *Deuteronomy*
  Recounts God's mighty deeds;
Brave *Joshua*, into Canaan's land,
  The hosts of Israel leads.
In *Judges*, their rebellion oft
  Provoked the Lord to smite,

The Books of the Old Testament—*Continued*

But *Ruth* records the faith of one
  Well pleasing in His sight.
In *First and Second Samuel,*
  Of Jesse's son we read.
Ten tribes, in *First and Second King's*
  Revolted from his seed.
The *First and Second Chronicles*
  See Judah captive led,
But *Ezra* leads a remnant black
  By princely Cyrus' aid.
The city walls of Zion,
  Nehemiah builds again,
While *Esther* saves her people
  From the plots of wicked men.
In *Job* we read how faith can live
  Beneath affliction's rod,
And David's *Psalms* are precious songs
  For every child of God.
The *Proverbs* like a goodly string
  Of choicest pearls appear;
Ecclesiastes teaches men
  How vain are all things here.
The mystic *Song of Solomon*
  Exalts sweet Sharon's rose,
Whilst Christ, the Saviour and the King,
  The "rapt" *Isaich* shows.
The warning *Jeremiah*
  The Apostate Israel scorns,
His plaintive *Lamentations*
  Their awful downfall mourns.
Ezekiel tells, in wondrous words,
  Of dazzling mysteries;
Whilst kings and empires yet to come,
  Daniel in vision sees.
Of judgments and of mercy, too,
  Hosea loves to tell,
Joel describes the blessed days
  When God with man shall dwell.
Among Tekoa's herdsmen
  Amos received his call,
Whilst *Obadiah* prophesies
  Of Edom's final fall.

The Books of the Old Testament—*Continued*

Jonah displays a wondrous type
　Of Christ, our risen Lord,
Micah pronounces Judah lost—
　Lost, but again restored.
Nahum declared on Ninevah
　Just judgments shall be poured.
A view of Chaldea's coming doom,
　Habakkuk's visions give.
And *Zephaniah* warns the Jews
　To turn, repent, and live;
Haggai wrote to those who saw
　The temple built again,
And *Zechariah* prophesied
　Of Christ's triumphant reign.
Malachi was the last who touched
　The high prophetic chord;
Its final notes sublimely show
　The coming of the Lord.

The Books of the New Testament

Matthew, Mark, Luke and *John*
Tell what by Christ was said and done;
Acts both of the Apostles tell,
And how the Holy Spirit fell.
Romans, Corinthians and *Galatians*,
Hard by *Ephesians* take their stations.
Then the *Philippians* hand in hand,
With the *Colossians* take their stand
By *Thessalonians;* each and all,
Claim for their author great St. Paul,
Who next writes twice to *Timothy*,
Then *Titus* and *Philemon* see
While *Hebrews* the last letter claims.
Next comes the *Epistle of St. James*,
While *Peter, John* and good *St. Jude*
With *Revelation* both conclude.

The Number Test

This is an impossible feat for any one who has not learned the number code. If you have mastered your code it is easy. It is excellent practice and creates intense interest in public or private entertainment.

Lesson Seven

The following twenty numbers and their locations can be remembered through the use of the code words:

1— 39	6— 42	11— 49	16— 34
2— 28	7— 63	12— 94	17— 74
3— 52	8— 55	13— 32	18— 82
4— 29	9— 48	14— 60	19— 36
5— 45	10— 69	15— 84	20— 73

These numbers are now changed into their corresponding code words and associated as follows:

1— 39
Hat associated with *Mop*
2— 28
Hen associated with *Knife*
3— 52
Ham associated with *Lion*
4— 29
Hare associated with *Knob*
5— 45
Hill associated with *Rail*
6— 42
Shoe associated with *Rain*
7— 63
Cow associated with *Jam*
8— 55
Hive associated with *Lily*
9—48
Ape associated with *Roof*
10— 69
Woods associated with *Ship*
11— 49
Tide associated with *Rope*

12— 94
Tin associated with *Bear*
13— 32
Team associated with *Moon*
14— 60
Tire associated with *Cheese*
15— 84
Hotel associated with *Fire*
16— 34
Dish associated with *Hammer*
17— 74
Dog associated with *Car*
18— 82
Dove associated with *Fan*
19— 36
Tub associated with *Match*
20— 73
Nose associated with *Comb*

Begin with Hat and You can Recall Every Picture Accurately in Order

The **Hat** brings to mind the picture of the **Hat** being used as a *Mop*, or whatever picture of these two objects you may have formed.

Mop is your code word for 39. Hence **39** is the number which is opposite **1**.

Hen recalls *Knife*, the code word for 28. Thus you know that **28** is opposite **2**.

Ham gives you *Lion*, the code word for 52. Therefore you know that **52** is opposite **3**.

LESSON SEVEN 285

In the same manner proceed right through the list and recall every picture. This will give you all the numbers in regular order.

You can call the numbers out of order also. You may be asked to give the number opposite 12. The picture you made with **Tin** was *Bear,* therefore **94** is opposite **12.**

Also Reverse the Process

You can also reverse the process. Suppose you wish to recall the position of 82. This is *Fan* and recalls your picture of *Fan* and **Dove.** Therefore **82** is opposite **18.**

If asked to locate 73, you know the code word for 73 is *Comb.* This brings to mind the picture of *Comb* and **Nose.** Therefore **73** is opposite **20.**

A little practice will enable you to place such figures in mind, regardless of the order in which they may be called.

As soon as you know your hundred words and their corresponding numbers, it will be good practice for you to ask your friends to test you with lists of numbers. At first take only five or ten numbers, and as you grow more proficient increase your tests.

In every instance you picture two objects, one representing the number called, and the other its code word location.

By reviewing your code words in their proper order you will be able to recall the entire list in order, either forward or backward.

At first take numbers between 1 and 100. Later take larger numbers, forming word combinations or single words for them, as explained in Lesson Five.

Additional Code Words

Confusion in remembering the smaller numbers can be avoided by learning the following list of *supplementary words,* representing numbers 1 to 20:

1—Tie	11—Dude
2—Honey	12—Den
3—Home	13—Dome
4—Arrow	14—Deer
5—Wall	15—Doll
6—Watch	16—Ditch
7—Key	17—Duck
8—Ivy	18—Dive
9—Pie	19—Depot
10—Toes	20—News

These words do not take the place of your code words, but are of use to represent numbers. If **5** were given you as the number to be placed opposite **1**, you would now associate *Hat* and *Wall*.

If you used your code word *Hill* to represent **5** in this instance and associated *Hat* and *Hill* you might become confused. Later you would not know whether this picture was intended to represent **1** opposite **5**, or **5** opposite **1**.

To Forget

Many people say that they wish to forget, rather than remember. This is often said jokingly, but at times there are things that we all wish to forget.

You have seen that every time you recall a mental record it becomes stronger and more firmly impressed in the mind. You have also learned that by denying any attention to your temporary mental pictures after they have served their purpose, they will pass out of your mind. In this way your code words are left free for filing other facts.

Direct Your Thoughts

This same principle can be used to remove disturbing thoughts. Refuse them any attention. Do not dwell on them. Every time you recall the circumstances you impress them more deeply on your mind. Therefore drive these thoughts away by denying them admission.

When these troublesome thoughts present themselves shut them out by thinking of something else. In this way you can reduce the keenness of many troubles and actually forget others.

Mind is Supreme

You can bring your mind under such control that it can dwell on any subject you please. Your code words and other lists in these lessons are invaluable for acquiring this freedom of mental action. By devoting a few minutes daily to these lessons, you will gain not only a better memory, but an ability to forget, and a mind under control.

SUMMARY

1—Application of the Number Code.
2—Three Things are Necessary.
3—Telephone Numbers and Exchanges.
4—Price Lists and Business Statistics.
5—Stop Payments on Checks.
6—Convenient Methods.
7—Perpetual Calendar.
8—Card Feats.
9—The Chess Knight's Tour.
10—History Dates.
11—Chemistry Aids.
12—Helps for Bible Students.
13—Memory Rhymes.
14—Number Tests.
15—To Forget.

Printed in the United States
94276LV00003B/39/A